Compliments of
KKXX 930AM
CHRISTIAN RADIO

Mrs. Pat Prather
1630 Timber Ln
Paradise, CA 95969

Spiritual Gifts

D1616307

by

David Hocking

Spiritual Gifts

Copyright 1992 by *Promise Publishing Co.*
                Orange CA 92667

Edited by M. B. Steele
Artwork by Mark Soderwall

Printed in the United States of America

ALL RIGHTS RESERVED. No part of this publication may be reproduced, stored in a retrieval system or transmitted in any form or
any means, electronic, mechanical, photo-copying or otherwise without the prior, written consent of the publisher.

Scripture is from The Holy Bible, New King James Version
Copyright 1984 by Thomas Nelson, Inc., Publisher

Library of Congress Cataloging-in-Publication Data

        Hocking, David
                Spiritual Gifts
ISBN 0-939497-28-X

ABOUT THE AUTHOR

David Hocking was raised in Southern California in a family where God was honored. His father was in the oil business during the exciting days of discovery and development of that industry in Southern California. Both of his parents have since "graduated to glory" but they left him a legacy of dependence on God and His Word that has stood David in good stead as a minister of the gospel.

His formal education includes his graduation (magna cum laude) from Bob Jones University, and degrees from Grace Theological Seminary and Graduate School, the California School of Theology and an honorary degree from Biola University. Although he values his education highly, David would be the first to tell you that "God puts the cookies on the bottom shelf" and he would encourage you to study God's Word for yourself believing that you don't have to have degrees in higher education to understand God's will for your life.

He and Carole, his wife, were married in 1962 and their home was blessed with three children, who are now married and have further enriched their lives with grandchildren. David has pastored in Long Beach, California, Columbus, Ohio and now serves as pastor of Calvary Church of Santa Ana, California.

His interest in radio dates back to 1974 when he was speaker on "Sounds of Grace" radio. In 1982, he became speaker of the Biola Hour broadcast. His radio rallies in various cities have resulted in seeing many people come to know Jesus Christ as Savior in addition to teaching God's Word in many areas of our country and in Canada. He has also travelled in other countries, carrying the gospel and teaching God's Word wherever he goes.

In 1991, he stepped into his own radio ministry called "Solid Rock Radio" headquartered in Orange, California. His ministry takes as its motto the hymn, "On Christ the Solid Rock I Stand". This is in keeping with his unswerving dedication to the Bible and to the gospel of Jesus Christ as it is taught in the Word of God.

INTRODUCTION

The subject of Spiritual Gifts has been a divisive topic in the Church of Jesus Christ. It is a great relief to those who are called "Charismatics" as well as those who consider themselves to be "Non-Charismatics" that the differences have become more accepted and less tension-filled in recent years. In spite of the doctrinal differences, it seems that Christians have finally realized that we have a great deal in common whatever our position on Spiritual Gifts such as the death, burial and resurrection of Jesus Christ, the inspiration of the Word of God and salvation by faith in Christ. Such tenets of faith we hold in common, and this should be the basis of our fellowship and cooperation in reaching out to the unsaved population of our earth.

This is not to say that there is no value in studying Spiritual Gifts or in pursuing a better understanding of them. Any study of God's Word is "profitable" and to be valued among us. We can differ in our understanding without giving up our recognition of each other as fellow believers and as brothers and sisters in Christ. In fact, it is good to know what people believe about Spiritual Gifts whether or not we see things exactly as they do. By knowing what is understood about the gifts, we are more apt to come to an understanding of what we believe ourselves. Certainly studying God's Word is a valuable use of our time.

Especially in areas in which we disagree to some extent or other, we must come to such a study all the more carefully, remembering that WE are not the authority - only God's Word is the authority and as we understand what God is saying, we will draw closer to one another as well as to our Heavenly Father and His Beloved Son. So, let us remind ourselves constantly that our experience, our understanding, our "position" in regard to Spiritual Gifts is not the criterion for what we believe. The Bible is God's message to us and He makes plain what we are to know about Him; however, we must apply ourselves to dig out the gems of truth He has buried for those of us who are willing to search for them.

I encourage you NOT to take my word for the teaching of the Bible about gifts, but to study these things for yourself. You will never be sorry about the time and effort you spend in this way. In fact, I believe it will enrich your Christian life and experience in a wonderful way.

Of course, when it comes to Spiritual Gifts, we are not content just to know what the Bible says about them. We take that knowledge and use it to discover our own Spiritual Gift so that we can exercise it according to the Bible. I urge you to spend the time necessary to get the complete background on this topic before embarking on this undertaking. There are pre-requisites to finding your gift, and using your gift will be much more effective when you implement it in light of a full understanding of Bible teaching. However, when you are ready, you will find major help in this discovery process included in this book. May your study be rewarding and your gift be effective in the service of our Savior.

David Hocking

TABLE OF CONTENTS

ABOUT THE AUTHOR
INTRODUCTION

CHAPTER	TITLE	PAGE
1	Historical Perspective	1
2	Principles of Body Life	6
	- Authority	7
	- Maturity	15
	- Unity	19
	- Diversity	22
3	Four Greek Words for Gifts	23
4	The Purpose of Spiritual Gifts	30
5	The Nature of Spiritual Gifts	38
6	Wrong Attitudes About Spiritual Gifts	42
7	How Many Gifts Are There?	45
8	Special Gifts	54
9	Speaking Gifts	68
10	Serving Gifts	78
11	Support Gifts	96
12	Sign Gifts	102
13	Discovering Your Gift	138
14	Testing For Your Gift	141

Historical Perspective

As each one has received a gift, minister it to one another, as good stewards of the manifold grace of God. If anyone speaks, let him speak as the oracles of God. If anyone ministers, let him do it as with the ability which God supplies, that in all things God may be glorified through Jesus Christ, to whom belong the glory and the dominion forever and ever. Amen (I Peter 4:10-11).

An Overview

In order to encompass the subject of "Spiritual Gifts", an overview is needed to see them fully and completely. Too many people have tried to look at Spiritual Gifts without understanding their functions and their intended purpose. Such fragmented studies tend to leave the student with a warped view in one way or another. We will try to avoid this pitfall and examine the subject as carefully as possible.

Of course, we have the New Testament accounts of Spiritual Gifts in the first century Church, but we also have some historical records which we can incorporate into our thinking on this subject. Perhaps this will give us a wider setting for our understanding and make it easier for us to see the Spiritual Gifts as they were understood by Christians in the early church.

Gifts in the Early Church

The use of Spiritual Gifts was found among other religious groups besides the early Christians. There was a notable emphasis on gifts among Gnostics and Montanists. Since Christians saw these groups as being outside the *"household of faith"*, they were skeptical of spiritual gifts for the first two hundred years of early church history. In other words, Christians were critical of those who used the gifts because of the perception of errant doctrine being linked with the use of spiritual gifts. Spiritual Gifts were not popularly sought after and those who exercised them were subjected to scrutiny as to motive, integrity of use as well as the source of the powers demonstrated. As Paul commended, the early Christians sought *"a more excellent way"* and they were characterized by their love for one another.

In A.D. 215, Hippolytus wrote a great deal about the Holy Spirit and Spiritual Gifts in his work, "Apostolic Tradition". In this volume which is still in existence, he refers to his treatise entitled, "On Charismatic Gifts" which has since been lost. He wrote during a century in which a hierarchy among clergymen rose. Along with and concurrently to the added layers of the clergy, there was a predictable de-emphasis on the laity and their gifts. Hippolytus took a stand against these trends and encouraged laymen to be more involved in the church and to exercise their Spiritual Gifts.

Other writers of that period were Irenaeus (who died in A.D. 200) and Origen who wrote in 254 A.D. Both of these church leaders referred to Spiritual Gifts and wrote of the "problem of tongues", but to a lesser extent than Hippolytus.

Gifts Prior to the Protestant Reformation

Twelve hundred years passed from the Council of Nicea until the Protestant Reformation. Many of the church writers made reference to the spiritual gifts in this period. Generally these writers dealt with the subject as a part of the overall activity of the church and did not place undue emphasis on the gifts. They were given a place of importance without overshadowing any of the basic doctrines of the Church.

Bishop Ambrose of Milan, who died in A.D. 397, wrote briefly on tongues in his treatise, "On the Holy Spirit". One of his chief contributions was his emphasis on the Bible teaching that every believer has a spiritual gift. Thus began the move away from the clergy/layman dichotomy that had developed along with the heirarchy of the church leadership. Believers in the pews were again called upon to exercise Spiritual Gifts as full, active members of the Church.

John Chrysostom of Antioch referred to "glossolalia" (the gift of speaking in tongues) as being scriptural, but as having ceased in his day. He died in A.D. 407. Without a complete treatise on the subject, however, we are left to draw whatever conclusions make sense to us from the brief references he gave.

St. Augustine was Bishop of Hippo. In his writings, he referred repeatedly to "tongues" and the gifts. He died in A.D. 430. Again, he did not leave us a logical brief of his complete views of the subject, so we are left to draw whatever inferences we can from the comments he did make.

Venerable Bede, who died in A.D. 735, also referred to the gift of tongues. Centuries later, Thomas Aquinas (A.D. 1247 is the date of his death) wrote about the gift of tongues and felt that it could be acquired in his day by linguistic study. This seems to represent a shift in thinking in regard to Spiritual Gifts which (at least on the surface) seems to contradict the very name of the topic. Perhaps he would have called them "Study Gifts" instead of "Spiritual Gifts".

However, the sum total of references to spiritual gifts leads us to conclude that they were not highly emphasized. Relative to the writings on other subjects, there is not a great deal that was written about Spiritual Gifts through the centuries of the Christian Church. It is also clear that the large majority of references that do appear deal with the gift of "tongues" and only to a lesser degree are other gifts discussed.

Gifts in Recent Centuries

Martin Luther wrote of the gifts of the Holy Spirit, and held that believers could receive one or several of the gifts. However, he stood against fanaticism and did not hold with people who "wanted to be everything", as he stated it. This view was against the backdrop of a highly organized church which held great power politically as well as economically. In his references to "tongues", he made it clear that he believed they were a sign given as a "witness to the Jews". He did not claim them for either the clergy or the laity of his day. He, too, would have said that tongues had ceased. He lived until A.D. 1546.

John Calvin wrote extensively on the gift of tongues; however, he believed this gift had been abused. He felt that God had removed them from the church rather than to have them violated by further abuse. Calvin was a contemporary of Martin Luther and would have joined him in the conclusion that tongues had ceased. He lived until 1564.

There was a renewed emphasis on the gifts that accompanied the appearance of the Camisards who were Prophets of the Cevennes Mountains of France. They lived during the time of Louis XIV. Their understanding of prophecy led them to expect a recurrence of the gift of tongues and they were certain that Joel's prophecy was taking place at that time. Words like, *"I will pour out My Spirit on all flesh; Your sons and daughters shall prophesy"*, and *"I will pour out My Spirit in those days"* enflamed their thinking concerning Spiritual Gifts.

Prior to her death in 1784, Ann Lee Stanley founded the Shaker Movement in which the gifts of the Spirit were practiced. This movement appears to have had roots back to the Camisards who were fanatical and extremely demonstrative in their use of the gifts. John Wesley was her contemporary, living until A.D. 1791. He preached "a second work of grace" and thus became known as the "father" of the Pentecostal Movement. Although he taught that Spiritual Gifts were available for believers, he never claimed to have any special gift himself. It seems clear that he did not equate Spiritual Gifts with spiritual maturity.

In the century that followed, Edward Irving, a Scottish Presbyterian preacher, began preaching a restoration movement of the spiritual gifts for the church. Prior to his death in 1834, this issue split the church, but his work continued after his death under the name of the "Catholic Apostolic Church".

About the same time, Joseph Smith (who led the Mormon Church) believed in and practiced the Gifts of the Spirit until his death in 1844 A.D. This practice was an essential part of his claim to have received additional revelation directly from God just as the Apostles' claims to direct revelation were accompanied by the Sign Gifts. If Joseph Smith were to claim new revelation effectively, he needed the same Sign Gifts to support his contention that the disciples had.

Gifts in the Twentieth Century

Modern Pentecostalism was started by Charles F. Parham in Topeka, Kansas in 1900 A.D. Five years later, he moved to Houston, Texas where he met William Seymour. Seymour picked up his teaching on the gifts and later when he moved to Los Angeles, he was active in what was called the Azusa Street Revival which began in 1906. This movement set the country ablaze with religious fervor and captured the attention of people all across America and around the world.

From the diversification which followed, ten denominations united to form the Pentecostal Fellowship of North America in1948. This exciting growth and activity produced many churches in many places. This was true to such an extent that later, a worldwide Pentecostal Fellowship was established. After a few years of relative isolation, keeping to themselves, the move toward Spiritual Gifts and their exercise began to crop up among the orthodox churches.

On April 3, 1960, Father Dennis Bennett, Rector of an Episcopal Church in Van Nuys, California announced that he had spoken in tongues. This event marks the birth of the Neo-Pentecostal Movement which crosses denominational lines, reaching into all denominations and with participants from all of them. Thus, there began a "charismatic movement" among the Episcopalians, the Presbyterians, and many other denominations. Current interest within the Roman Catholic Church continues to emphasize the importance of this movement.

The Pentecostal Movement is largely responsible for the interest in Spiritual Gifts that has grown in the twentieth century. Usually where we find the exercise of Spiritual Gifts, there is an emphasis on "tongues" and "healings" to the exclusion of other gifts although there are clearly many more gifts than these to be found in Scripture. The general subject of "Spiritual Gifts" has captured the interest of many churches and church leaders both Charismatic and Non-Charismatic. There are underlying reasons that contribute to the unflagging interest in Spiritual Gifts; for example, the de-personalization of secular society creates a need in most people to know and understand their personal worth and value.

With the presence of a strong, well-trained clergy, the need for lay people has once again come into question. In the local churches, the question often is, "Do we care about

people?" and "Are lay people needed in the growth and ministry of the church?" Both of these questions must be answered with a loud, "Yes!"

Not only is it impossible for clergymen to carry the load of the many people who look to them for help, but there are many needs of people which can only be met by those who are involved in their personal lives. The clergy cannot extend far enough into the level of their needs to do more than offer words of encouragement and guidance. Many needs can only be met by the personal touch of a friend. Spiritual Gifts offer many ways to minister at this level.

Summary of the History of Spiritual Gifts

From this brief overview, we see that the use of Spiritual Gifts declines when the role of lay persons is reduced. During the Middle Ages there was a lack of biblical teaching concerning spiritual gifts. This resulted in a failure to understand or to use Spiritual Gifts. When the clergy takes over the performance of the ministries of Spiritual Gifts, lay people seem to lose the desire to use them. They often back away from them at such times.

At other times in history, the fanaticism and emotional display connected with the use of Spiritual Gifts has discouraged many churches and kept them from identifying with the need for and the use of Spiritual Gifts. Also, the exalting of certain gifts over others tends to diminish the importance and use of the other gifts.

The evidence of pride and the lack of balanced teaching is clear from the historical point of view. This has been demonstrated by the fact that there was teaching on tongues even at times when the other gifts were not taught, nor even mentioned. However, when the clergy understands their function to be the encouragement and development of Spiritual Gifts among the people, use of the Gifts will grow and thrive.

Bible teaching (as well as history) demonstrates that leaders are responsible to teach and train their people in the use of Spiritual Gifts. The responsibility rests on their shoulders!

Principles of Body Life

When we come to the study of Spiritual Gifts, we see from the outset that these are to be exercised by those who name the name of Christ; that is, the Church. The definition of Spiritual Gifts has to do with people who are influenced by and have been *"made alive"* by the Holy Spirit. Such a definition coincides with the definition of a believer: those who have come to faith in the Lord Jesus Christ by the work of the Holy Spirit. Thus, when we talk about the exercise of Spiritual Gifts, we are talking about the activities of the people who make up the Body of Christ — the Church. Simply put, the Church is people who know and follow Jesus Christ.

AUTHORITY

Jesus Christ = The Head

The Need for Direction and Control

In considering how the physical body works, we see clearly that certain principles apply. For instance, our bodies must be under our control if they are to function well and accomplish the things we set out to do. When a person is unable to control his body, we say he has a handicap—and that is certainly true. Without control, we would be unable to function toward the end that our wills and our minds have chosen.

When we are joined with other believers in the Body of Christ, we come under His control since Scripture clearly teaches that He is the Head of the Church.

> *But I want you to know that the head of every man is Christ, the head of woman is man, and the head of Christ is God (I Cor. 11:3).*

We may not want to accept all that this verse implies; that is a discussion for another time and place. Nevertheless, this verse makes it very clear that Christ is our *"head"*. There are other verses, perhaps less controversial, which also make the same statement. Speaking of God, Paul writes of the power ...

... which He worked in Christ when He raised Him from the dead and seated Him at His right hand in the heavenly places, far above all principality and power and might and dominion and every name that is named, not only in this age but also in that which is to come. And He put all things under His feet, and gave Him to be head over all things to the church, which is His body, the fullness of Him who fills all in all (Eph. 1:20-23).

God has placed Jesus Christ as head of the Church, and He is referred to by that name in Ephesians 4:15 and other verses:

... may grow up in all things into Him who is the head—Christ—from whom the whole body, joined and knit together ... according to the effective working by which every part does its share (Eph. 4:15-16).

And He is the head of the body, the church ... (Col. 1:18).

You are complete in Him, who is the head of all principality and power (Col. 2:10).

Scripture leaves no doubt that Jesus Christ has been given the authority to head up the church by God Himself.

Besides the illustration of Jesus as the head of the body (the church), we also see that salvation comes from Him.

To each one of us grace was given according to the measure of Christ's gift (Eph. 4:7).

The verses that follow go on to show how Jesus Christ uses His power and authority as the head of the Church.

Therefore He says: "When he ascended on high, He led captivity captive, And gave gifts to men." (Now this, "He ascended"—what does it mean but that He also first descended into the lower parts of the earth? He who descended is also the One who ascended far above all the heavens, that He might fill all things.) And He Himself gave some to be apostles, some prophets, some evangelists, and some pastors and teachers (Eph. 4:8-11).

Salvation ministered to believers by the Holy Spirit was obtained by the sacrifice of Christ on the cross. Just as the Holy Spirit is an integral part of our salvation, He is also an integral part of the gifts given to us by the Savior.

Since our salvation was gained for us by Christ and since He is the One who gives gifts to men, then it follows that Jesus Himself is to be the object of glory and praise.

If anyone speaks, let him speak as the oracles of God. If anyone ministers, let him do it as with the ability which God supplies, that in all things God may be glorified through Jesus Christ, to whom belong the glory and the dominion forever and ever. Amen (I Peter 4:11).

We are specifically warned here against using the gifts to glorify ourselves or to deliver our own messages. The Spiritual Gifts are given:

—to deliver God's message

—by means of God's power and ability,

—that God may be glorified through Jesus Christ.

There is no other legitimate use of the Spiritual Gifts. These are God's abilities which He distributes to His people by His Spirit to accomplish His work.

Scripture reminds us repeatedly that none of this is to be done without Jesus Christ Himself.

Now, therefore, you are no longer strangers and foreigners, but fellow citizens with the saints and members of the household of God, having been built on the foundation of the apostles and prophets, Jesus Christ Himself being the chief cornerstone, in whom the whole building, being joined together, grows into a holy temple in the Lord, in whom you also are being built together for a habitation of God in the Spirit (Eph. 2:19-22).

For no other foundation can anyone lay than that which is laid, which is Jesus Christ (I Cor. 3:11).

Besides the illustration of the body and the head, Jesus is pictured as the cornerstone of our faith. He is also called the Lord of the servants. Jesus said,

"Most assuredly, I say to you, a servant is not greater than his master; nor is he who is sent greater than he who sent him" (Jn. 13:16).

Therefore I make known to you that no one speaking by the Spirit of God calls Jesus accursed, and no one can say that Jesus is Lord except by the Holy Spirit. There are differences of ministries, but the same Lord (I Cor. 12:3, 5).

Therefore God also has highly exalted Him and given Him the name which is above every name, that at the name of Jesus every knee should bow, of those in heaven, and of those on earth, and of those under the earth, and that every tongue should confess that Jesus Christ is Lord, to the glory of God the Father (Phil. 2:9-11).

The authority of Jesus Christ is taught on the pages of the Bible and we can see it there, if we will only look.

How To Recognize and Submit to Christ's Authority

In the early days of the church, there were many decisions to be made—many new situations to deal with, and the apostles set some examples for us which show us how to find and follow the Lord Jesus Christ as He leads us.

Then the twelve summoned the multitude of the disciples and said, "It is not desirable that we should leave the word of God and serve tables. Therefore, brethren, seek out from among you seven men of good reputation, full of the Holy Spirit and wisdom, whom we may appoint over this business; but we will give ourselves continually to prayer and to the ministry of the word" (Acts 6:2-4).

Here we have two criteria—prayer and God's Word. Thus, we seek to recognize the authority God has given Jesus Christ by praying. This certainly finds support in the words of Jesus.

"And whatever you ask in My name, that I will do, that the Father may be glorified in the Son. If you ask anything in My name, I will do it (Jn. 14:13-14).

Jesus makes Himself the point of contact where we are to go with our requests so that God, the Father, may be glorified. He offers not only to hear our requests, but also to give us the answers we seek. Moreover, He challenges us to ask Him for more than we have ever asked before, and He promises us joy along with His answers.

"Until now you have asked nothing in My name. Ask, and you will receive, that your joy may be full" (Jn. 16:24).

Paul also pointed to prayer as the means of receiving what we need. He saw it as an outgrowth of lives of obedience and loving service to Jesus Christ.

And whatever we ask we receive from Him, because we keep His commandments and do those things that are pleasing in His sight (I Jn. 3:22).

Now this is the confidence that we have in Him, that if we ask anything according to His will, He hears us. And If we know that He hears us, whatever we ask, we know that we have the petitions that we have asked of Him (I Jn. 5:14-15).

The other way we come to know Jesus and to submit to His authority is through the study of His Word and the application of what we learn to our lives.

If you instruct the brethren in these things, you will be a good minister of Jesus Christ, nourished in the words of faith and of the good doctrine which you have carefully followed (I Tim. 4:6).

And a servant of the Lord must not quarrel but be gentle to all, able to teach, patient, in humility correcting those who are in opposition, if God perhaps will grant them repentance, so that they may know the truth, and that they may come to their senses and escape the snare of the devil, having been taken captive by him to do his will (II Tim. 2:24-26).

All Scripture is given by inspiration of God, and is profitable for doctrine, for reproof, for correction, for instruction in righteousness, that the man of God may be complete, thoroughly equipped for every good work (II Tim. 3:16-17).

We find in God's Word all that we need to live the lives that God has set before us. Nonetheless, we are not to sit in church and hear what is said without applying the truth to our lives every day.

But be doers of the word, and not hearers only, deceiving yourselves. For if anyone is a hearer of the word and not a doer, he is like a man observing his natural face in a mirror; for he observes himself, goes away, and immediately forgets what kind of man he was. But he who looks into the perfect law of liberty and continues in it, and is not a forgetful hearer but a doer of the word, this one will be blessed in what he does (James 1:22-25).

The Work of the Holy Spirit

The Holy Spirit is the One by whom Christ ministers to the members of His body—the church. His first function in this regard is to form the body of Christ.

For by one Spirit we were all baptized into one body—whether Jews or Greeks, whether slaves or free—and have all been made to drink into one Spirit (I Cor. 12:13).

So, it is by the Holy Spirit that we become part of Christ's body and from that point, He controls and fills the hearts and lives of believers.

And do not be drunk with wine, in which is dissipation; but be filled with the Spirit (Eph. 5:18).

I say then: Walk in the Spirit, and you shall not fulfill the lust of the flesh
(Gal. 5:16).

Paul put this concept in every way imaginable in his writings. The comparison with being *"drunk with wine"* is crystal clear in showing that the Spirit of God is to permeate every part of our being and take control of our lives to the point of our no longer having control over what we do and say. Paul also points out that this is our greatest defense against self-centeredness and sin.

It is possible that a believer might fail to profit from having Christ in his life. However, to the believer who allows himself to be controlled by the Holy Spirit there comes the fruit of His presence.

But the fruit of the Spirit is love, joy, peace, longsuffering, kindness,
goodness, faithfulness, gentleness, self-control. Against such there is no
law (Gal. 5:22-23).

Not only is the believer filled with the fruit of having the Holy Spirit in his life, but the Holy Spirit also uses him to minister to the needs of other members of the body.

But the manifestation of the Spirit is given to each one for the profit of all
(I Cor. 12:7).

As each one has received a gift, minister it to one another, as good
stewards of the manifold grace of God. If anyone speaks, let him speak as
the oracles of God. If anyone ministers, let him do it as with the ability
which God supplies, that in all things God may be glorified through Jesus
Christ, to whom belong the glory and the dominion forever and ever. Amen
(I Peter 4:10-11).

So it is clearly seen that the Holy Spirit ministers through a member of Christ's body to other members of the body so that all may bring glory to God through Jesus Christ. This is the means by which the Holy Spirit edifies and builds up the body of Christ.

Now hope does not disappoint, because the love of God has been poured
out in our hearts by the Holy Spirit who was given to us (Rom. 5:5).

The entire 13th chapter of I Corinthians explains how the love of God works to direct, cleanse and build our lives in a manner pleasing to God. Then, the ultimate work of the Holy Spirit in the body of Christ is to bring about the reproduction of believers through the work of believers. The Holy Spirit uses the body to witness to the world.

"A new commandment I give to you, that you love one another; as I have loved you, that you also love one another. By this all will know that you are My disciples, if you have love for one another" (Jn. 13:34-35).

"But you shall receive power when the Holy Spirit has come upon you; and you shall be witnesses to Me in Jerusalem, and in all Judea and Samaria, and to the end of the earth" (Acts 1:8).

The Ministry of the Holy Spirit in the Body of Christ

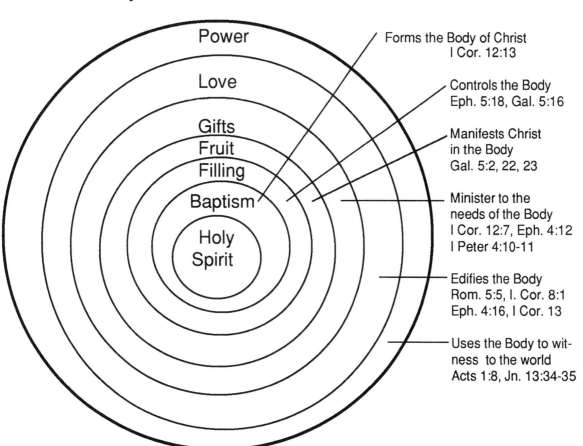

MATURITY

The second principle of body life is that it needs to grow and develop.

The following chart outlines the stages of spiritual growth that are described in the Bible and briefly what is characteristic of each stage. Each one is given a specific name and each has a spiritual need which can be met by the ministry of the Holy Spirit. Place yourself in this list and check the dangers and problems which you are experiencing. Then, read the Scripture given to help you find God's answer to your problem until you move to a stage of spiritual maturity.

Don't tell me that you have been a Christian for thirty years, however, because you don't automatically reach spiritual maturity because of the passing of time. Some new believers grow by leaps and bounds and reach an amazing level of maturity in a short time. Other believers have been known to sit in the pew for years with no visible change. Be sure to erase from your consideration any maturity you have laid claim to on the basis of longevity.

LEVELS	SPIRITUAL NEED	DANGERS/PROBLEMS
BABIES	ASSURANCE I John 2:12	Inability to understand and use spiritual gifts due to age.
TODDLERS	DISCERNMENT Heb. 5:11-14 Eph. 4:14	Immaturity in using gifts due to lack of doctrine and/or carnal living.
CHILDREN	DISCIPLINE I John 2:13-14 Heb. 12:5-11	Insensitivity toward others when using your gifts due to lack of experience and suffering.
YOUNG PEOPLE	VICTORY I John 2:13-14	Ineffectiveness in using gifts due to sinful practices.
PARENTS	REPRODUCTION I John 2:13-14	Inactivity in using your gifts due to wrong priorities or disobedience toward spiritual responsiblities.

Personal Study of the Bible

There are three ways to develop spiritual maturity in the life of the believer. The first one we have already looked at as we saw the pattern of problem solving that the apostles set for us. They gave themselves to the study of God's Word and this is the means by which we, too, can become mature believers. There is no substitute for this exercise of faith. We need to know what God has told us in His Word and our lives should be washed every day in His truth.

> *Be diligent to present yourself approved to God, a worker who does not need to be ashamed, rightly dividing the word of truth (I Tim. 2:15).*

This Scripture was not written to preachers and theologians but to each one of us. It is our business to know God's Word and be able to handle it in a way that pleases Him.

> *But as for you, continue in the things which you have learned and been assured of, knowing from whom you have learned them, and that from childhood you have known the Holy Scriptures, which are able to make you wise for salvation through faith which is in Christ Jesus. All Scripture is given by inspiration of God, and is profitable for doctrine, for reproof, for correction, for instruction in righteousness, that the man of God may be complete, throughly equipped for every good work (Tim 3:14-17).*

> *As newborn babes, desire the pure milk of the word, that you may grow thereby, if indeed you have tasted that the Lord is gracious (I Peter 2:2-3).*

The Discipline of Suffering

The Christian's attitude toward suffering is not easily explained to new believers or to unbelievers yet Paul dealt extensively with how we are to react to and handle suffering that comes to us in this life.

> *And not only that, but we also glory in tribulations, knowing that tribulation produces perseverance; and perseverance, character; and character, hope. Now hope does not disappoint, because the love of God has been poured out in our hearts by the Holy Spirit who was given to us (Rom. 5:3- 5).*

> *And you have forgotten the exhortation which speaks to you as to sons: "My son, do not despise the chastening of the Lord, Nor be discouraged*

when you are rebuked by Him; For whom the Lord loves He chastens, And scourges every son whom He receives." If you endure chastening, God deals with you as with sons; for what son is there whom a father does not chasten? But if you are without chastening, of which all have become partakers, then you are illegitimate and not sons. Furthermore, we have had human fathers who corrected us, and we paid them respect. Shall we not much more readily be in subjection to the Father of spirits and live? For they indeed for a few days chastened us as seemed best to them, but He for our profit, that we may be partakers of His holiness. Now no chastening seems to be joyful for the present, but grievous; nevertheless, afterward it yields the peaceable fruit of righteousness to those who have been trained by it (Heb. 12:5-11).

This is not a stray idea that was thrown in to keep us patient in adversity. This is written out for us so that we can understand that suffering is one of the means by which the Holy Spirit accomplishes the work of Christ in our lives. It is presented again and again and in great clarity.

My brethren, count it all joy when you fall into various trials, knowing that the testing of your faith produces patience. But let patience have its perfect work, that you may be perfect and complete, lacking nothing (James 1:2-4).

God tells us to be glad when we find ourselves up to our necks in hot water. We are to fix our eyes on the end result and we are to accept the pain of the trial knowing that the Holy Spirit is at work.

But may the God of all grace, who called us to His eternal glory by Christ Jesus, after you have suffered a while, perfect, establish, strengthen, and settle you. To Him be the glory and the dominion forever and ever. Amen (I Peter 5:10-11).

The Ministry of Spiritual Gifts

As believers minister their spiritual gifts on behalf of one another, spiritual growth is stirred up.

He Himself gave some to be apostles, some prophets, some evangelists, and some pastors and teachers, for the equipping of the saints for the work of ministry, for the edifying of the body of Christ, till we all come to the unity of the faith and the knowledge of the Son of God, to a perfect man, to the measure of the stature of the fullness of Christ; that we should no

longer be children, tossed to and fro and carried about with every wind of doctrine, by the trickery of men, in the cunning craftiness by which they lie in wait to deceive, but, speaking the truth in love, may grow up in all things into Him who is the head-Christ-from whom the whole body, joined and knit together by what every joint supplies, according to the effective working by which every part does its share, causes growth of the body for the edifying of itself in love (Eph. 4:11-16).

Here we see the full circle. God gave spiritual gifts to some to be apostles and other kinds of ministers so that the saints would be equipped for the work of ministering. This ministering accomplishes the edification (building up) of faith and knowledge of Jesus Christ so that other saints can become mature believers and carry on the work that builds the body of Christ.

Even so you, since you are zealous for spiritual gifts, let it be for the edification of the church that you seek to excel (I Cor. 12:14).

The Purpose is Maturity and Growth

This is not just doctrinal maturity. This is knowledge by experience and by fact put together. Notice what Paul writes:

"... we all come to the knowlege of the Son of God, to a perfect man, to the measure of the stature of the fullness of Christ; that we should no longer be children" (Eph. 4:13-14).

That word *"children"* is *"nepios"* in Greek; it means *"a child without speech"*. It refers to a toddler who can't construct his sentences very well as yet.

... that we no longer be children (toddlers) tossed to and fro and carried about with every wind of doctrine, by the trickery of men, in the cunning craftiness by which they lie in wait to deceive (Eph. 4:14).

UNITY

There is in the body of Christ, a unity that is not found anywhere else. It is a spiritual unity only approximated by the closeness of ideal family life. The following chart lays out for us the areas of unity given to us in the Bible and describes the purpose for each one. Check yourself to see if you are fulfilling each point so that you can contribute to *"the unity of the Spirit in the bond of peace"*.

Scripture	Meaning
ONE BODY	The PURPOSE we all should have in ministering to one another.
ONE SPIRIT	The POWER behind the gifts in terms of source and operation.
ONE HOPE	The PROSPECT which motivates us and makes it all worthwhile.
ONE LORD	The PERSON we really serve and whose life we manifest.
ONE FAITH	The PREREQUISITE in being a part of the body and having spiritual gifts.
ONE BAPTISM	The POSITION we now have as a member of the body and the importance we have to one another.
ONE GOD AND FATHER	The PREEMINENCE of God the Father in all we are and all we do.

All of these are found in our key Scripture:

I, therefore, the prisoner of the Lord, beseech you to have a walk (a lifestyle) worthy of the calling with which you were called, with all lowliness and gentleness, with longsuffering, bearing with one another in love, endeavoring to keep the unity of the Spirit in the bond of peace. There is one body and one Spirit, just as you were called in one hope of your calling; one Lord, one faith, one baptism; one God and Father of all, who is above all, and through all, and in you all (Eph. 4:1-6).

Responsibility

Without question, we are told in these first phrases that we ARE responsible for the way in which we live, and we are challenged here to live our lives worthily. It's great to know that we are "The King's Kids", but there's more to it than that! We are expected to live as children of the King of kings and Lord of lords. What we do and say, and how we do things and how we say things are important. We will be held responsible for our lives.

Reactions

I have heard people try to absolve themselves from feelings of guilt for their actions by saying, "I can't help how I feel about things!" God seems to think that you CAN help it and He tells us how to react to the pressures and trials of life.

First, we are to accept what comes to us in humility (*"lowliness"*). When something happens to us that we don't like, we say, "I didn't deserve that!" I contend that if we got what we deserve, we would all wind up in hell. We are sinners and we deserve to be punished. The fact that God has provided salvation for us through Jesus Christ is an amazing miracle which we do not deserve.

Compared to that, what else matters? Did you get a dent in your fender? Well, look at it this way—if you have a dent in your fender, then you have a car; do you deserve that? Did someone get promoted over you? Were you the one who was laid off? Were you rejected or betrayed by someone important in your life? Do you think you didn't deserve that? If you were left behind in a promotion, then you have a job; do you deserve it? If you were laid off, then you will be able to work when you find a job; do you deserve good health? If you have been rejected, then you have known the joy of love at some time; did you deserve to be loved?

If we are humble, we know that we don't deserve any of the good things of life. All that we have ever enjoyed has been the result of God's grace and love toward us. We have no grounds on which to demand, or even to expect anything from God. If He chooses to bless us, it is on the basis of His love - not on the basis of our merit.

Next, we are to react with *"gentleness"* because Jesus was gentle.

"Come to Me, all you who labor and are heavy laden, and I will give you rest. Take My yoke upon you and learn from Me, for I am gentle and lowly in heart, and you will find rest for your souls. For My yoke is easy and My burden is light" (Matt. 11:28-30).

Finally, patience is to characterize our reactions. It is described as one of *"the riches of His goodness"*. God has patiently sought us in order to give us His marvelous gift of salvation, how then can we refuse patience to those who need it?

> *Or do you despise the riches of His goodness, forbearance and longsuffering (patience), not knowing that the goodness of God leads you to repentance? (Rom 2:4).*

> *The Lord is not slack concerning His promise, as some count slackness, but is longsuffering toward us, not willing that any should perish but that all should come to repentance (II Peter 3:9).*

Relationships

We are to *"bear with one another"* in our relationships, and it is not to be done grudgingly, but in love. What a difference this will make in our lives and our homes! It means that we hang in there with each other during the hard times and remain loyal even when we don't deserve it. This has to be a divine gift—it certainly isn't human!

Finally, we are to work at keeping unity and peace. The importance of maintaining the unity of the Spirit cannot be overstated. That doesn't mean that we agree with everything we're told, but it does mean that we don't start a war over it! If changes are necessary, they are to be encouraged without recrimination and fighting. If we're challenged to a fight, we're to decline—in love—whenever possible.

The Goal is Unity

> *... for the edifying of the body of Christ, till we all come to the unity of the faith and the knowledge of the Son of God, to a perfect man, to the measure of the stature of the fullness of Christ (Eph. 4:12-13).*

The little word "till" is a Greek word *"mechri"* which has the idea of a goal. The goal of edification is the unity of the faith. This is not talking about everybody being Christians—that would be evangelism.

One of the reasons for edification is so that we'll have "unity in the faith" in terms of what we believe. Instead, we see much disunity. One reason this is happening is that individual Christians are not edifying each other. They are not building each other up. They are to be the protective shield—the defense against the enemy.

We should all be encouraging a brother when we see he's discouraged. Let's don't let him fend for himself; let's don't let him sulk all week in his misery. Let's go to him,

and encourage him in the Lord. When we see someone who is sick and suffering and we have the Gift of Showing Mercy, let's go to him and minister to him. God equipped us to do this with compassion and love and they need us desperately.

When some brother doesn't know what to do and he's wondering about his failing marriage and the other problems in his family, any among us with the Gift of Exhortation and Counsel should be "Johnny-on-the-spot" to help him. We must all be involved in this ministry in order for it to occur. If we all were helping, the "unity of the faith" would be more of a reality.

DIVERSITY

Later on, we'll deal with the great diversity of Spiritual Gifts and their uses. For the moment, suffice it to say that the body of Christ (like our physical bodies) performs various work by means of the unique abilities of the individual parts. We walk with our feet because they are better at it than walking on our hands. We see with our eyes because that is the function for which they were created. Our hands are marvellously created to take care of a great divergence of tasks, but not everything!

Some parts hold positions of honor and glory. Some are protected and covered. This is as it is in the body of Christ as well. Not everyone is gifted by God to be the spokesperson seen by all. Some are given positions of such sensitivity that they must be protected and covered. Some parts are for routine jobs and others for highly specialized work.

Nevertheless, it must be recognized that every part is essential and none can replace the other. An eye cannot be used to hold the knife that chops the onions, and an ear cannot be expected to appreciate color and shape. Moreover, each one needs the other for the hands cannot perform a task unless the feet carry them to the place where it is to be done. Can the hands say to the feet, "I don't need you!" Of course not! Every part is necessary and each one needs the other. Every member of the body of Christ is unique, essential and to be valued.

Four Greek Words for Gifts

Now concerning spiritual gifts, brethren, I do not want you to be ignorant: You know that you were Gentiles, carried away to these dumb idols, however you were led. Therefore I make known to you that no one speaking by the Spirit of God calls Jesus accursed, and no one can say that Jesus is Lord except by the Holy Spirit.

Now there are diversities of gifts, but the same Spirit. There are differences of ministries, but the same Lord. And there are diversities of activities, but it is the same God who works all in all. But the manifestation of the Spirit is given to each one for the profit of all; for to one is given the word of wisdom through the Spirit, to another the word of knowledge through the same Spirit, to another faith by the same Spirit, to another gifts of healings by the same Spirit, to another the working of miracles, to another prophecy, to another discerning of spirits, to another, different kinds of tongues, to another the interpretation of tongues.

But one and the same spirit works all these things, distributing to each one individually as He wills (I Cor. 12:1).

When you ask the question, "What is a spiritual gift?", there are four ways to answer. There are four words translated "gift" in English, all of which are referring to this subject. What is a spiritual gift? It is four things.

The Initial Gift

The number one spiritual gift is the work of the Holy Spirit by which we become Christians. There is a particular Greek word that is used to describe that kind of gift. This word refers to the Spirit himself—the word *"dorea"*. In Greek it refers to a free gift.

This free gift is salvation, in particular, the ministry of the Holy Spirit by which we become members of the family of God. Let me show you the usage of this word translated *"gift"* in our English Bible. It was in the message of Peter on the Day of Pentecost.

Then Peter said to them, "Repent, and let every one of you be baptized in the name of Jesus Christ for the remission of sins; and you shall receive the gift of the Holy Spirit" (Acts 2:38).

That is not something outside of the Spirit; *"... the gift of the Holy Spirit"* means the Holy Spirit Himself, especially His work by which we become Christians.

In the household of Cornelius, when the gospel was introduced to Gentiles, something unexpected occurred.

While Peter was still speaking these words, the Holy Spirit fell upon all those who heard the word. And those of the circumcision who believed were astonished ... because the gift of the Holy Spirit had been poured out

on the Gentiles also. For they heard them speak with tongues and magnify God. Then Peter answered, "Can anyone forbid water, that these should not be baptized who have received the Holy Spirit just as we have?" (Acts 10:44-47).

Later, Peter recounts the story:

"And as I began to speak, the Holy Spirit fell upon them, as upon us at the beginning. Then I remembered the word of the Lord, how He said, 'John indeed baptized with water, but you shall be baptized with the Holy Spirit.' If therefore God gave them the same gift as He gave us when we believed on the Lord Jesus Christ, who was I that I could withstand God?"

When they heard these things, they became silent; and they glorified God, saying, "Then God has also granted to the Gentiles repentance to life".

It's clear in Acts that being baptized with the Holy Spirit is the same thing as receiving *"the gift of the Holy Spirit"* and it happened when they believed. It's talking about receiving salvation, becoming a part of the family of God and the phrases are used interchangeably.

This is the Spiritual Gift that we talk about as the initial gift. Before any other gift you receive, you must receive the presence of the Holy Spirit in your life. You cannot, therefore, excercise a spiritual gift unless you're a believer. You must first of all receive the Holy Spirit, who in turn imparts His power and ministry through your life.

Spiritual Gifts are not simply abilities that we acquire through education or training, etc. That's why playing the piano is not a Spiritual Gift. You can learn how to play the piano. You cannot learn how to use a Spiritual Gift in the sense of acquiring that gift. You may hone it, sharpen it up because of your knowledge of the Word, but you either have a gift or you don't, and no one who is an unbeliever has a Spiritual Gift.

Let's kill the theory that some Christians have, that we're born with our gifts and as we get older, we learn how to use them. They think that it doesn't really make any difference whether we're Christians or not. That's a very important point as you look at some of the gifts, because some of the gifts mentioned in the Bible are claimed by those who are not Christians. Even false religions and cults are involved in the ministry of the gifts of the Bible, and it's very important to understand from the start that the work of the Holy Spirit by which we become Christians is the initial gift, the free gift of eternal life, of salvation.

It is the baptism of the Holy Spirit by which we become members of the body of Christ.

No one is a Christian who does not have the Holy Spirit.

Now if anyone does not have the Spirit of Christ, he is not His (Rom. 8:9).

We're talking about being born again.

You are baptized by the Spirit;

you receive Him as a gift into your life,

and then He will distribute gifts through your life.

Gifted Men in the Church

Spiritual gifts also refers to gifted men whom Christ gave to the church to equip the other believers for ministry. This is the word, *"doma"*. This is a beautiful working process by which God has built His church and enabled it to minister.

But to each one of us grace was given according to the measure of Christ's gift (Eph. 4:7).

It's interesting the last word *"gift"* is the word *"dorea"*, the initial gift. When you become a Christian you receive the free gift of salvation—the person of the Holy Spirit. To each one of us, grace (literally *"the grace"*, meaning the one shown through Jesus Christ when He died on the cross) has been given to each one of us, and the measure of this gift which we have is related to the gift of Christ himself in providing everlasting life—unlimited, inexaustible. Whatever ability we Christians have received to minister for the Lord is the result and product of the marvelous grace of our Lord Jesus Christ that was seen at the cross when Jesus died.

Therefore he says: "When He ascended on high, He led captivity captive, And gave gifts to men" (Eph. 4:8).

There's our English word *"gift"*. It is not the word *"dorea"* nor is it the word *"charisma"* meaning charismatic gifts. It's the word *"doma"*. It means *"the thing that is given"* and that is explained in the next verses.

And He Himself gave some apostles, some prophets, some evangelists, and some pastors and teachers, for the equipping of the saints for the work of ministry, for the edifying of the body of Christ (Eph. 4:11-12).

The Bible says that pastors and teachers are for equipping the saints for the work of serving or ministering. We should all be serving the Lord. What does the work of ministering or serving mean?

> As each one has received a gift, minister it to one another, as good stewards of the manifold grace of God ... that in all things God may be glorified through Jesus Christ. (I Peter 4:10-11).

All of us are supposed to minister and serve, and the pastors and teachers are supposed to equip us so we can do it, and the result of our doing it is that the body of Christ is built up. So the pastor-teacher is only indirectly building up the body of Christ. Actually, we build each other up as we minister for the Lord.

The gifts we are given are products of God's grace, and God has given them to us even though we don't deserve them — that's the meaning of grace. He gives us something we do not deserve and we are stewards; we manage the many kinds of things that God's grace gives to us. We each have gifts we're to administer to one another. The text teaches clearly that it is God's words we minister and that the glory all goes to Jesus Christ. What is the work of ministry? It is the use of spiritual gifts, and when we use our gifts, the body of Christ is built up.

Ephesians 4:16 goes on to say that the body of Christ is built up in the sphere of love —if you don't love, you can't use your gift properly. That's why I Corinthians 13 is found between chapters 12 and 14 which deal with gifts. Right in the middle is the greatest chapter ever written on love. We are to minister our gifts with love to each other, and as a result, we all get stronger. It is incorrect theology to think that you can be alone, isolated from other Christians, and be thoroughly built up in the Lord. That is not taught in the Scriptures.

The great tragedy in the body of Christ is so many of us try to make it on our own. We act like we don't need each other. That simply is not true. That is not what the Bible teaches, and we suffer at some point in our Christian experience when we try to ignore our dependency upon other believers. God speaks against those attitudes. We are to minister our gifts to each other, to build each other up.

You may ask the question, how are people equipped for ministry? The answer is,"By the Word of God". Pastor-teachers are to teach us the Bible—the Word of God, Scripture, doctrine, reproof, correction, instruction and righteousness so we'll be equipped to minis-ter, to use our spiritual gifts in the body of Christ. Very important!

The Bible calls Levites who worked in the tabernacle of God *"gifted men for the ministry of the tabernacle"*. In the Old Testament economy, there were gifted people to train, teach, and guide the people of God just as surely as there are people to do those things today in the New Testament church. God has always worked on that principle.

"Behold, I Myself have taken your brethren the Levites from among the children of Israel; they are a gift to you, given by the Lord" (Num. 18:6).

In the Greek Old Testament, that's the word *"doma"*, the exact same word that is in Ephesians 4:8. You have the same exact thing in the New Testament—God has given gifted men.

A lot of people get in trouble over spiritual gifts because they've forgotten the ministry of the gifted men who equip them so they can do the work of ministering. They find out they have a gift and they try to use it without remembering that they need to be equipped in the Word of God. A lot of people fail, or misunderstand, or abuse the ministry of gifts because they do not see the importance of being equipped. You are not spiritual (or Spirit-filled) because you have a gift. The church at Corinth had all of the gifts according to I Corinthians 1:7, and they were a carnal church.

You may have all of the gifts, but that does not make you a spiritual Christian. It is possible to be wicked and carnal, and still have the gifts, so it's very important to understand the equipping process. If you want to build up the members of the body of Christ using your gift, make sure you understand what the Scripture teaches about equipping the body of Christ so that the ministry is what God really intended. It must be done in the sphere and understanding of the Word of God as it teaches us how to use our gifts.

Miraculous Deeds

The Bible uses the word *"gift"* to describe the miraculous deeds used in the time of the apostles to prove that their message was truly from God, but the word for *"gift"* is not *"dorea"* (The Initial Gift); it is not *"doma"* (The Gifted Men). It's not even the word *"charisma"* for charismatic gifts. It is the word *"merismos"* which means to divide. The noun is used twice in the New Testament. As a verb, it's used fourteen times. It means to divide and it's translated *"gift"*.

"Therefore, we must give the more earnest heed to the things we have heard, lest we drift away. For if the word spoken through angels proved steadfast, and every trangression and disobedience received a just reward, how shall we escape if we neglect so great a salvation, which at the first began to be spoken by the Lord, and was confirmed to us by those who heard Him, God also bearing witness both with signs and wonders, with various miracles, and gifts ("merismos", dividings) of the Holy Spirit, according to His own will?" (Heb. 2:1-4).

First, Jesus speaks the gospel, the salvation message of eternal life. Jesus speaks it. He tells about it.

Next, the ones who heard Him (the apostles) tell "us" (those who heard at the time of the writing of Hebrews thirty years later). The apostles are telling "us", but how do those who heard the apostles telling the Gospel thirty years later know that they truly heard Jesus?

The answer of Hebrews 2 is that we know they heard Him because of the signs wonders and miracles (*"gifts of the Holy Spirit"*) that they did. God worked the *"signs and wonders"* to prove that their message was truly from God. When we talk about gifts, we ARE referring to miraculous deeds which were used in the time of the apostles to prove that their message was truly from God.

Special Abilities

Spiritual gifts also refer to the special abilities given to each believer by the Holy Spirit for the benefit of others. This is the word *"charisma"*.

Don't say that your spiritual gift is being used when you are alone. That simply is not taught in the Bible. God gives you a gift to benefit someone else. There is no "private" gift. If God gave you a spiritual gift, He gave it so you could help other members of the body of Christ. He gave it for the benefit of other people besides yourself, and if you think of it only in terms of yourself, you have a very selfish idea of the gifts — different from the one taught in the Scripture.

THE PURPOSE OF SPIRITUAL GIFTS

Equipping of the Believers

And He Himself gave some to be apostles, some prophets, some evangelists, and some pastors and teachers, for the equipping of the saints (all believers) for the work of ministry (using spiritual gifts), for the edifying (or building up) of the body of Christ Eph. 4:11-12).

What is equipping? The method by which we equip people to use their spiritual gifts is by the Word of God.

All Scripture ... is profitable for doctrine, for reproof, for correction, for instruction ... [so] that the man of God may be complete, thoroughly equipped for every good work (II Tim. 3:16-17).

The story is told in Matthew 4:18-22 of Jesus' calling James and John to be His disciples. They were mending their fish nets when He called them. The word *"mending"* (Matt. 4:21) is the exact same word as the word *"equipping"* in Ephesians 4:12.

They had dropped their nets into the water, and they had pulled in fish. According to Jesus, fish are a sign or symbol for reaching people for Christ. He said, *"Follow Me, and I will make you fishers of men."* To fish for men means to reach people for Christ and introduce them to Jesus. Fishermen used nets and sometimes they broke with the weight of the fish. They had to mend the nets in order to use them to fish again. *"Mending"* is the word *"equipping"*. Apostles, prophets, evangelists and pastor/teachers are to *"equip"* the believers (*"mend the nets"*) so we can catch more fish.

I was in Korea a few years ago. I was met at the airport and they said, "David, we need you to speak". They did not know me and yet I was to substitute for a speaker who was not able to come. There was an interpreter. I was thinking of one speaking assignment, but they meant six times a day for one week. They had two musical groups, but only one speaker - ME ! All week long I had just enough strength to get into the next bus and go to the next "opportunity". In one week, I spoke to over 200,000 people and saw over 20,000 people come to Christ. I say that to God's glory—to prove a point. I didn't have any sermons prepared. I just pulled sermons out of the old barrel. I just got up there and talked; I told people about Jesus. God was working on His timetable and His schedule.

You have a gift, I have a gift and we are to use them to build each other up in the Lord. Every believer is important in the ministry of gifts. We all have a ministry to do. Every single one of us. To the extent that we are ministering to each other, that is the extent to which "the net is mended" and can be used to catch the fish that God wants to catch.

In Exodus, we're told about the Tabernacle and the garment of the high priest.

> *"It shall have two shoulder straps joined at its two edges, and so it shall be joined together" Ex. 28:7).*

One day I was reading that passage in the Greek Old Testament and I saw that the word *"equip"* (Eph. 4:12) is used for *"joined together"*. It may seem insignificant to you, but Ephesians 4:12 says that pastor teachers are to *"join the members together"* so they minister one to another.

That's equipping.

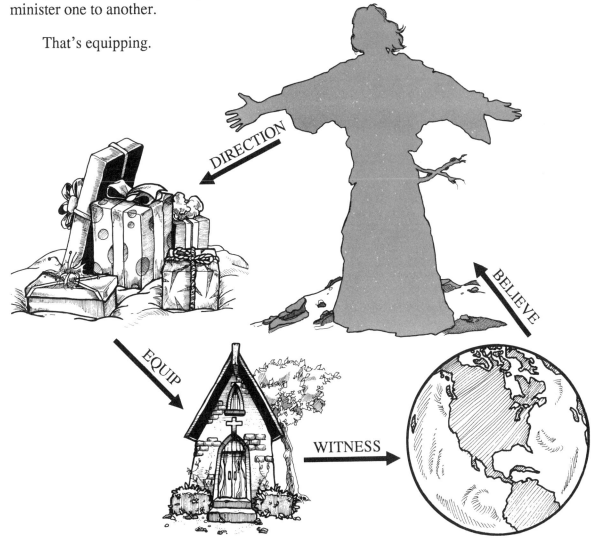

Equipping Is For The Accomplishment of Every Good Work

Equipping is important not only for the edification of the body of Christ, but also for the accomplishment of every good work that God wants us to do. No matter what you can describe as being a good work, in order for believers to do it, equipping is necessary.

> *All Scripture (every writing) is given by inspiration of God (God breathed), and is profitable for doctrine (teaching), for reproof, for correction, for instruction in righteousness, that the man of God may be complete, thoroughly equipped for every good work (II Tim. 3:16-17).*

To be *"equipped"*—complete, thoroughly equipped for every good work, we must have constant input from the Scriptures. Every Scripture is inspired of God and profitable to equip us so that we all can be able to do *"every good work"*. There's also an inference here that where the good works of the believers break down, it may be that they are not being equipped. There is the necessity of constant input from God's word.

Equipping Is For Restoration

> *Brethren, if a man is overtaken in any trespass, you who are spiritual restore (that's our word "equip") such a one in a spirit of gentleness, considering yourself lest you also be tempted (Gal. 6:1).*

"Overtaken" has the idea of continuing in a sin. It's a sin that has a hold on someone; it's controlling them. The Bible says that those who are spiritual (Spirit-filled, walking with the Lord) are to *"equip"* (*"restore"*) them.

Attitude is important here. It is not to be done with an attitude of spiritual superiority, but a spirit of gentleness. *"Considering yourself, lest you also be tempted."* Gentleness is meekness. It's the opposite of revenge. We need to have the right spirit. We're not to club people who are sinning. If God is going to work in their life and rebuild it, we need to come with love and forgiveness and understanding.

As we deal with a sinning brother, we are also warned to be very careful lest we also are tempted in the same area. There are two ways to take that. One is that we need to be careful lest our attitude is so bad toward the sinning brother, we would be tempted to sin in the matter of attitude. There's also the possibility that the last phrase is saying, be careful lest you become involved in the very sin that you're trying to deal with.

We do need to restore sinning brothers. We need to go to a brother or sister who has fallen into sin, and attempt to restore them and to *"equip"* them. Equipping is necessary,

and equipping is done by the Scriptures. People need God's Word; they need it in order to be restored and to rebuild their lives from a pattern of sin.

Equipping Is For Strengthening Our Faith

> *For what thanks can we render to God for you, for all the joy with which we rejoice for your sake before our God, night and day praying exceedingly that we may see your face and perfect ("equip") what is lacking in your faith? (I Thess. 3:9-10).*

These were brand new believers. There is a very important time of equipping in the life of the believer when he is lacking in faith, confidence and trust before God, and because of immaturity, may not be able to use his gift to build up other brothers and sisters. We all need to be equipped in God's Word so that our faith gets stronger and we're able to trust God and to believe His Word.

Equipping Is For Doing God's Will

The material of our lives needs to be joined together. This word was used of joints out of place, being put back into place. Our joints need to be put into place. We need to shape up—that's what the Scripture is saying. We need to be equipped by the Scriptures, so we'll shape up and become a well-oiled, hard-working machine for God. We're to use our gifts the way He wants, and one of the things God wants is that we do His will. We all need to be *"equipped"* in order to do His will.

> *Now may the God of peace who brought up our Lord Jesus from the dead, that great Shepherd (pastor) of the sheep, through the blood of the everlasting covenant, make you complete (equipped) in every good work to do His will, working in you what is well pleasing in His sight, through Jesus Christ, to whom be glory forever and ever (Heb. 13:20-21).*

Equipping Is For The Unity of Believers

> *Now I plead with you, brethren, by the name of our Lord Jesus Christ, that you all speak the same thing, and that there be no divisions among you, but that you be perfectly joined together ("equipped") in the same mind and the same judgment (I Cor. 1:10).*

So it occurs to me that *"equipping"* is also for the unity of the believers. If we really stick to God's word, we have an openness and transparency about us that allows people to say in kindness and love what needs to be said to help us and to make us more effective.

Equipping is for the unity of the believers which is so vital to the ministry of gifts and the effect of our testimony upon the world.

Equipping Is For The Manifestation of Christ-likeness

"A disciple is not above his teacher, but everyone who is perfectly trained (equipped) will be like his teacher" (Luke 6:40).

In Hebrews 13, the writer says, *"May God equip you through the great Shepherd of the sheep"*. Pastor-teachers are equipping believers, but the great Shepherd is the One who is actually equipping us through the Word so that ...

we will live like Him,

act like Him,

talk like Him.

"Let your light so shine before men, that they may see your good works and glorify your Father in heaven" (Matt. 5:16).

It is God who commanded light to shine out of darkness who has shone in our hearts to give us the light of the knowledge of the glory of God in the face of Jesus Christ. But we have this treasure in earthen vessels, that the excellency of the power may be of God and not of us (II Cor. 4:6-7).

When we are equipped, when God's Word begins to take hold of our lives, we'll see God's Word controlling our actions, and pretty soon, we start seeing Jesus. They said of Peter and John, unlearned men who had not been to the rabbinical schools of their day, *"They have been with Jesus."*

Edification of the Whole Church

As each one has received a gift, minister it to one another, as good stewards of the manifold grace of God (I Peter 4:10).

... for the equipping of the saints for the work of ministry, for the edifying (edification) of the body of Christ (Eph. 4:12).

In a local church, the pastor-teacher is to equip the people to use their gifts in order to build up the body. Without equipping, the ministry of spiritual gifts does not accomplish building each other up.

I really feel a sense of loss and failure as a pastor, if, in the teaching of God's Word, those who hear never do anything with it. I am not simply a walking information booth. I am a motivator of people.

If I do not give you something to share with someone else, then I have failed.

If I don't equip you to use what you have for the Lord, I have failed.

If I don't equip you to use what you've learned for the Lord, I have failed.

If I don't motivate you to share what you know with someone else, I have failed.

If I don't motivate you to build up someone else, I have failed—we have all failed.

God wants us to edify one another—to build each other up. The equipping of God's Word is for that reason—so that we have something to share as we use our gifts.

Encouragement of the Believers

One of the gifts God has given us is the gift of exhortation, encouragement or comfort depending on the translation you're reading.

It's interesting that even though there's one special Gift of Encouragement, the Bible teaches that any spiritual gift imparted can result in encouragement. That is one of the purposes of the gifts.

This is the only verse in the entire Bible where the word *"spiritual"* and the word *"gifts"* are put together. In I Corinthians 12, we see these words, but that's just in English, it's not in Greek. All it says in I Corinthians 12 is, *"now concerning spiritual things"*. It doesn't mention gifts at all.

> *For I long to see you, that I may impart to you some spiritual gift, so that you may be established—that is, that I may be encouraged together with you by the mutual faith both of you and me (Rom 1:11-12).*

When you go to minister to people, do you ever discover that they often minister to you instead? Paul said that we're *"encouraged together"*. Often, when you minister to somebody who's sick, you find they minister to you.

Exaltation of Jesus Christ

As each one has received a gift, minister it to one another, as good stewards of the manifold grace of God. If anyone speaks, let him speak as the oracles of God. If anyone ministers, let him do it as with the ability which God supplies, that in all things God may be glorified through Jesus Christ, to whom belong the glory and the dominion forever and ever. Beloved, do not think it strange concerning the fiery trial which is to try you, as though some strange thing happened to you; but rejoice to the extent that you partake of Christ's sufferings, that when His glory is revealed, you may also be glad with exceeding joy (I Peter 4:10-13).

Even in suffering, when His glory is revealed we'll be *"glad with exceeding joy"*.

My whole attitude changes when I realize that the reason I'm here, and what God is doing through me..., my gifts..., my times of suffering, is to glorify Himself. That's why He made me.

The church at Corinth didn't *"come behind in any gift"*. They had them all, and they were working, but they were a carnal church. Insead of those gifts building each other up and being a blessing, they became a serious problem in the church of Corinth. They were not glorifying God; they were not exalting Jesus Christ.

We must ask ourselves, "How are we using our gifts? What are we doing with what God has given us? What is our motive behind it?"

God has given us gifts in order to exalt His Holy Name.

THE NATURE OF SPIRITUAL GIFTS

NEGATIVELY:

1. They are not the same as natural talents or abilities.
2. They are not the same as the "fruit" of the Holy Spirit.
3. They are not evidence of spiritual maturity and growth.
4. They are not given to you because you pray or ask for them.
5. They are not acquired abilities or talents which an individual is able to produce.

COMPARISON CHART	
1. Singular — "fruit"	1. Plural — "gifts"
2. Attitudes	2. Activities
3. No Carnality	3. Carnality possible
4. Affects yourself primarily	4. Affects others primarily
5. Main purpose is to control the flesh	5. Main purpose is to edify the body
6. All believers can possess all the "fruit"	6. All believers do not have the same gift, nor do they have all the gifts
7. The result of being controlled by the Spirit	7. The result of salvation and the sovereign distribution of the Spirit

But the fruit of the Spirit is love, joy, peace, longsuffering, kindness, goodness, faithfulness, gentleness, self-control. Against such there is no law (Gal. 5:22-23).

POSITIVELY:

1. They are the "manifestation of the Spirit".

But the manifestation of the Spirit is given to each one for the profit of all (I Cor. 12:7).

This is not a demonstration of personal intelligence or talent. The Spiritual Gifts are the expression of the life of the Holy Spirit inside your life. This removes all possibility of personal glory for whatever gifts you may have.

2. They are distributed by the Holy Spirit.

They are given to us by the sovereign will of the Holy Spirit. You can't pray and receive them; you can't ask and get them. You can't run around the church ten times and get them. They are given sovereignly by the Holy Spirit of God. He gives them according to what He wants to do.

One and the same spirit works all these things, distributing to each one individually as He wills (I Cor. 12:11).

Now God has set the members, each one of them, in the body just as He pleased (I Cor. 12:18).

God is doing what He wants to do. You can't do anything about it. What you have, you have. Some folks say, "I sure hope I have the Gift of Leadership. I'd like to run things." But if you've got the Gift of Helps instead of the Gift of Leadership, you are never going to make it.

Some who want the Gift of Leadership like to be in front of people and have them notice their gift. Well, anyone with the Gift of Leadership knows that it's no easy task. It's embarrassing. You're open to all kinds of criticism, and nobody ever agrees with you. It is very tough to be a leader.

Still, if you think leaders have trouble, you should see the administrators. They are different from the leaders. Everybody thinks administrators are hard as a rock, insensitive to people's needs. To be an administrator and still have the joy of the Lord takes some doing!

There are all kinds of gifts, but if you think you're going to get one that puts you in the limelight, you'd better forget it.   God has given you what He wants to give you. You're stuck with it, so you might as well enjoy it.

3. Every Believer Has At Least One Gift

Every believer has at least one gift. Some people say, "I have no gift. Poor, miserable me! I'm a worm of the dust. God gave me zero. I will never have a ministry." Oh, no! I'm not going to let you off the hook. If you're a believer in the Lord Jesus Christ, you have at least one gift. *"As each one has received a gift ...,"* says I Peter 4:10. I Cor. 12:7 says, *"It is given to each one "*. Every believer has at least one of these abilities; we call it *"charisma"*. The Greek word *"charis"* is grace, so you could also say that these are *"graces"*. Spiritual Gifts are *"graces"* from God to you. We don't deserve them, but every believer has at least one.

There are great differences, not only in the kinds of gifts that God gives, but also in the way that they are used.

> *Now there are diversities of gifts, but the same Spirit. There are differences of ministries, but the same Lord. And there are diversities of activities, but it is the same God who works all in all (I Cor. 12:2-4).*

Let's take the gift of teaching because this is one over which Christians disagree a little bit. The Bible says that some have the gift of teaching, some have the gift of leadership, some have the gift of serving and on and on. So there are differences in the number of gifts—*"diversities of gifts"*.

It also says there are *"differences of ministries"*. The way the gift is used varies. Is it possible that somebody could be good at teaching children, and not good at teaching adults? I know people who really think they can teach anybody, and I've seen them use their whole ministry on toddlers. I've seen some people who don't even believe they HAVE the gift of teaching deal with pre-school kids, and I say, "That is a miracle of God's grace! How do they do that?" The only answer is that God has given us gifts and they are different not only in the kinds of gifts, but also in the way that they are used.

There are also differences of activities, workings, our idea of energy. I think the point here is very important in the body of Christ. It's possible that some of us are good at teaching small groups (for example); maybe we're good with one-on-one or one-on-three, but in front of a large group, something happens. Some people can't do that. Sadly, some people get a bad self image and think they can't teach because they can't teach large groups.

Don't question the gift God has given you! Use it!

Don't wish it were greater ... or different ... allow God's "gifted men" to equip you to use it to the fullest!

> *It is the same God who works all in all (I Cor. 12:6).*

4. They are the result of God's grace—we do nothing to earn or to deserve them.

> Having *then gifts differing according to the grace that is given to us, let us use them (Rom. 12:6).*

There is an extensive variety of gifts since God gives to each of us according to His will and His grace. As many believers as there are, that is the limit to the diversity of gifts and abilities to use His gifts.

God's grace is shown in that He gives us gifts even though we are unworthy of carrying that honor. In addition, He shows His grace in that the gifts are to be used to minister to and bless others, so the grace extends beyond ourselves.

Do you wonder why you are here and what life is all about? Here's an answer that will stand up in the spotlight of eternity—you're here to minister the gift God has given you to those who are in need of it.

THE WORK OF GOD

in "Differences"
I Cor. 12:4-6

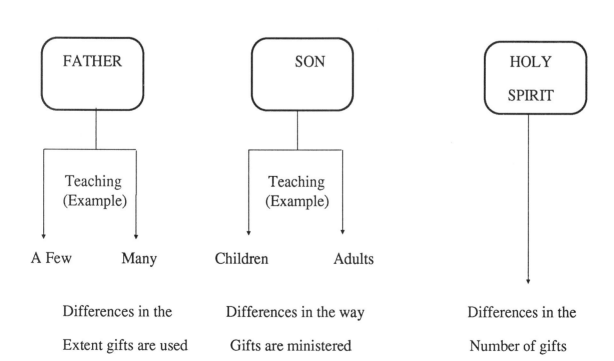

Wrong Attitudes About Spiritual Gifts

Before we go on to look at the Spiritual Gifts individually, we need to be sure that we are not carrying wrong attitudes with us into the study. They could be detrimental and spoil the effectiveness of your work in studying. To avoid this, let's look at the attitudes that might mislead us.

"All I Need to Know" Attitude

You may have studied Spiritual Gifts before and, if you have, you will know that "once around" was not enough. The fact that you are involved in this study shows that you have already discovered this. If you haven't studied the Spiritual Gifts before, you may not know that you won't learn all there is to know about Spiritual Gifts in this manual. I'd like to say that you could get it all here, but it just wouldn't be true. However, I like your enthusiasm! Nonetheless, we never "finish" studying God's Word. Other teachers and other studies will open your eyes to things you haven't seen this time through.

And YOU will change. As you grow in maturity, there will be additional light that God will shed on your studies. So don't consider this a one-time thing. Be ready and willing to come back to the subject again the next time you have an opportunity.

"I Can Be Used of God" Attitude

It is useful to search and find out what your Spiritual Gift is. It can help you to know the way in which God has blessed you so that you can be a blessing to others. But knowing your gift and having it useful and effective are two different things. Other factors that will affect the way God uses your gift are things like the status of the Holy Spirit's work in your life. If you are refusing to yield to Him and let Him work in your heart, He will not use your gifts in the full, mighty way that He would otherwise. If you fail to study God's Word, He is limited by that unwillingness in putting your gift to work in the church. You just plain won't know what you need to know to be a "sharpened tool" in God's hand.

Any time you let your commitment to God waiver or get lost in the daily grind, you will notice that God is not using your Spiritual Gift as He once was. Also it is sure that if you indulge in sinful practices, He will find you unusable and take from you the place of

ministry that you have enjoyed. There are lots of reasons why God doesn't use your gift. Sometimes He just chooses to do things some other way. So knowing what your gift is doesn't guarantee that God will give you a great work to do.

"I Am Spiritual" Attitude

Too many people equate the exercise of their Spiritual Gift with great, deep, wonderful spirituality. Sorry! Nice try! However, we have the illustration of the Church at Corinth where the believers were carnal, and yet they exercised ALL the Spiritual Gifts.

"I Am No Longer Responsible for Other Gifts" Attitude

So often, teachers (for example) will focus in on their teaching and exclude the other gifts. For instance, they won't want to help the neighbor with a broken leg whose lawn needs to be mowed—after all, their gift is Teaching, not Showing Mercy. Or consider the man who has the Gift of Giving, but never calls on the sick in the hospital. This is a wrong attitude in that we are all responsible to minister in each area of the gifts because of our Christian duty to one another, and because of our accountability to God.

There is a Gift of Prophecy; still, all believers are exhorted to prophesy. The same is true of the other gifts. There is a Gift of Knowledge, but all believers are told to study God's Word. There is a Gift of Showing Mercy even though all believers are to be typified by showing mercy and love. No, we cannot excuse ourselves from any Christian ministry on the basis that our gift lies elsewhere.

"My Gift Is For My Personal Benefit" Attitude

Especially in certain areas, people like to say that their gift is for their own edification and spiritual growth. In reading I Corinthians, however, it is made clear that the Spiritual Gifts are given for the benefit of others, not for ourselves.

> *But the manifestation of the Spirit is given to each one for the profit of all (I Cor. 12:7).*

> *Even so you, since you are zealous for spiritual gifts, let it be for the edification of the church that you seek to excel (I Cor. 14:12).*

"My Gift Can Only Be Used by the Power of the Holy Spirit" Attitude

We could wish this were true, but the Church at Corinth was not controlled by the power of the Holy Spirit, yet they had all of the Spiritual Gifts and they used them. To be sure, there seems no doubt that we will be more effective when using our Gifts under the control of the Holy Spirit.

The giving of the Gift is the work of the Holy Spirit, but the using of it is our responsibility. You can be "carnal" and still use your gift. You can use your gift without love, and the results may be disastrous! Here is a matter of deep concern for each of us. Let's examine ourselves and see HOW we are using our gifts.

"Spiritual Gifts Cause Pride" Attitude

Some people go to the other extreme and want to declare all Spiritual Gifts out-of-bounds because they are sometimes exercised outside of the power of the Holy Spirit. We need to separate in our minds, however, the conclusion that the carnality was CAUSED by the gifts from the fact that carnality was PRESENT where believers were exercising the gifts. The gifts can be very effective in bringing the church into spiritual maturity and love. The carnality was caused by a lack of love and the failure to be controlled by the Holy Spirit.

How Many Gifts Are There?

There are several lists of Spiritual Gifts given in the Bible which don't seem to agree on the surface. Some list only the gifts under discussion in that particular passage of Scripture and, even in the more comprehensive lists, none seems to be a complete list of Spiritual Gifts. In order to formulate a list of all the Spiritual Gifts, therefore, we must consider all the lists given in Scripture and compile our own list.

This is where we find a great deal of difference of opinion for Bible teachers seem never to find a standard list on which they can all agree. There are many influencing factors to help us determine what we want to include and/or exclude on our comprehensive list of Spiritual Gifts and this is how we determine the ultimate list. These factors will be identified as we move through the lists in order to help you see how I arrived at the gifts I put on my list.

The first list we'll consider is found in Ephesians.

> *And He Himself gave some to be apostles, some prophets, some evangelists, and some pastors and teachers (Eph. 4:11).*

That pastor/teacher is one person is a conclusion based on the Greek construction. Thus, there are four gifts listed in Ephesians 4:11.

One — apostles,

two — prophets,

three — evangelists,

and four — pastor/teachers.

The second list is in Romans:

> *For I say, through the grace given to me, to everyone who is among you, not to think of himself more highly than he ought to think, but to think soberly, as God has dealt to each one a measure of faith. For as we have many members in one body, but all the members do not have the same function, so we, being many, are one body in Christ, and individually members of one another. Having then gifts differing according to the grace that is given to us, let us use them: if prophecy (gift five), let us prophesy in proportion to our faith; or ministry ("serving"/"deacon" - gift six), let us use it in our ministering; he who teaches (gift seven), in*

teaching; he who exhorts ("counseling"/"rebuking"/"restoring" - gift eight), in exhortation; **he who gives (gift nine), with liberality;** *he who leads ("to stand before" - gift ten), with diligence; he who shows mercy (gift eleven), with cheerfulness (Rom. 12:3-8).*

But the manifestation of the Spirit is given to each one for the profit of all: for to one is given the word of wisdom through the Spirit (gift twelve), to another the word of knowledge through the same Spirit (gift thirteen), to another faith (gift fourteen) by the same Spirit, to another gifts of healings by the same Spirit (gift fifteen), to another the working of miracles (gift sixteen), to another prophecy (this one was already listed in Rom. 12), to another discerning of spirits (gift seventeen), to another different kinds of tongues (gift eighteen), to another the interpretation of tongues (gift nineteen). But one and the same Spirit works all these things, distributing to each one individually as He wills (I Cor. 12:7-11).

There are two Greek words translated *"another"*. One of them means *"another of the same kind"*; the other one means *"another of a different kind"*. Let me show you how they're used. When Paul says, *"... to another the word of knowledge"*, he uses the word *"another of the same kind"*. So, *"the word of knowledge"* is somehow **like** *"the word of wisdom"*. When you come to the fourteenth gift, *"to another faith"*, he changes the word to *"another of a different kind"*. There is some sense in which faith is **different from** *"the word of wisdom"* and *"the word of knowledge"*. What that difference is remains to be seen; we don't have the final explanation on this.

Gift fifteen is *"gifts of healings"*. Notice that the word *"gift"* is PLURAL, not singular. It's the only one in which the title of the gift has the plural word, *"gifts of healings"*. And the word *"healing"* is not singular either, but it is plural — *"healings"*, *"gifts of healings"*.

There are different ways to use a gift, and different ways in which healings take place. There are two Greek words for healing. One word is a broad word that could refer to emotional and spiritual healing. We get our word "therapeutic" from it. However, the word here means a definite, physical healing.

We've had four in a row which are **like faith** (*"another of the same kind"*), but when you come to tongues and interpretation, he changes the word again and says *"another of a different kind"*. So tongues are **different** from the five gifts preceding it. Why did he change the words? Those of us who believe in the infallibility and inspiration of the Bible, believe that none of the words of the Bible are unimportant. That makes this an important question.

One possibility is that those words are used interchangeably — *"another of the same kind"* and *"another of a different kind"*. That seems strange to me since they're so opposite.

Another possibility would be that there's a difference in the way each of these gifts function. That's a possibility.

Another difference might be, a difference in the purpose of each of those. That's another possibility. Which is right? I don't know.

"To another different kinds of tongues" - we have the plural again (*"kinds"*). That is our English word *"genealogy"* and is referring to various classifications. Here is the reason I believe the whole argument about ecstatic utterances breaks down. I don't believe that tongues can possibly be ecstatic utterances. I believe they're foreign languages. You wouldn't use the word *"genea"* in the plural (meaning kinds, classifications, generations, or families) of ecstatic utterances. However, we **would** use it when talking about foreign languages. The logical conclusion seems to be a reference to the ability to speak in several foreign languages without previous knowledge.

Next, it says *"to another of the same kind"* meaning that the interpretaton of tongues is like the kinds of tongues. The word *"interpretation"* is our English word *"hermeneutics"* which means the science or art of interpretation. It's used many times in the Bible for the simple word *"translation"*. So, we're talking about translating the languages that are spoken by the other person.

The list continues:

And God has appointed these in the church: first apostles, second prophets, third teachers, after that miracles, then gifts of healings, helps (gift twenty),

administrations (gift twenty-one), varieties of tongues (I Cor. 12:28).

Some say that *"helps"* is the same as the serving gift. Again trusting the infallibility and inspiration of the Scriptures, I believe that if God wanted us to believe *"serving"* and *"helps"* were the same, He would have used the same word in both passages. Since that isn't the case, I think there's a difference between the two.

The next word is *"administrations"*. This is another example of a different gift. I do not believe *"leadership"* (Romans 12) is the same as *"administrations"* (I Cor. 12). If God meant them to be the same, He would use the exact same word. He chose a different word.

Peter mentions the Gift of Hospitality:

But the end of all things is at hand; therefore be serious and watchful in your prayers. And above all things have fervent love for one another, for "love will cover a multitude of sins." **Be hospitable to one another (gift twenty-two)** *without grumbling. As each one has received a gift, minister it to one another, as good stewards of the manifold grace of God. If anyone speaks, let him speak as the oracles of God. If anyone ministers, let him do it as with the ability which God supplies, that in all things God may be glorified through Jesus Christ, to whom belong the glory and the dominion forever and ever. Amen (I Peter 4:7-11).*

Here's a paragraph about what we should do since we know that *"the end of all things is at hand"*. We're to be serious about prayer; we're to have fervent love for one another, and then it goes on to explain **how that love is expressed.** The next verse begins *"Be hospitable"*. It's a participle related to the *"fervent love"* mentioned before.

The word *"hospitable"* means *"loving strangers"*. It isn't necessarily having them over for dinner in your house, it could be the simple act of shaking someone's hand. It has to do with **not waiting for them to come to you,** but with your going to them. Some people are more outgoing, more gregarious; they like to meet people. That is a spiritual gift. At least, I think it's a good possibility even though not many people put this down in their lists of Bible gifts.

It says, *"... be hospitable to one another without grumbling. As each one has received a gift...."* Actually, this is all one sentence. The assumption of the grammar is that hospitality is a gift. The word *"as"* literally is *"just as"*. It must of necessity refer to the remark preceding it. *"Be hospitable ... just as each one has received a gift."* The obvious point is that hospitality is a gift, so let's add hospitality as gift twenty-two.

Some people add two more gifts here. It says, *"If anyone speaks, let him speak as the oracles of God. If anyone ministers, let him do it as with the ability which God supplies...."* I don't think these are two different gifts. First of all, if they were, it would be strange because then there would be several *"speaking"* gifts. Also, since the word *"minister"* is the same word *"serving"* that we saw in Romans 12, he's already mentioned it.

A better possibility here is that in summary, Peter is dividing all of the gifts into Speaking Gifts or Serving Gifts.

> *For I wish that all men were even as I myself. But each one has his own gift from God, one in this manner and another in that. But I say to the unmarried and to the widows: It is good for them if they remain even as I am (I Cor. 7:7).*

Paul's statement, *"I wish that all men were as I am"* means that he was once married. He even used the word *"unmarried"* when he could have used the word *"virgin"*, but he did not. He used the word that indicates that someone has been married, but isn't now (divorced or widowed).

So I believe that Paul was married, and his wife died; he was a widower. He's asking that everybody remain as he, if they can. If they can't, if they don't have self-control, then they should marry.

> *"For I wish that all men were even as I myself. But each one has his own gift from God".*

How interesting the word *"gift"* here is our word *"charisma"* — charismatic gifts. Let's add to our list *"celibacy"* (gift twenty-three). There is a gift (a spiritual gift) of celibacy, the ability to live as a single.

The other side of that is also true. He said, *"... one in this manner and another in that"*. It appears that there is also a Gift of Marriage (gift twenty-four). First of all, it's obvious that Paul calls this a charismatic gift. That's the word used in the text.

This also proves a point about Spiritual Gifts — you cannot get something you don't already have. One of the important points about spiritual gifts is whatever gifts you have, God gave them to you, and you can't get one you don't have by praying or seeking it from God. The Bible teaches that gifts are given to you sovereignly by the Holy Spirit. He distributes *"to whomever He will"* (I Cor. 12:11). Relax, don't panic over gifts. You

may not even know what your gift is, but the Holy Spirit is fully able to exercise it in your life even though you don't know.

SIGN GIFTS

*God also **bearing witness** both with signs and wonders, with varous miracles, and gifts of the Holy Spirit, according to His own will (Heb. 2:4).*

According to this text, there are gifts called *"signs, wonders and miracles"* which God used to confirm the spoken message of the apostles.

"And these signs will follow those who believe: In My name they will cast out demons (gift twenty-five); they will speak with new tongues (already listed); they will take up serpents; and if they drink anything deadly, it will by no means hurt them (the gift of physical protection); they will lay hands on the sick and they will recover" (Mk. 16:17-18).

Let's make *"physical protection"* gift twenty-six. There's some special ability here to be physically protected. You can take up a snake or drink something deadly, still *"it will by no means hurt them"*. Many people would like to speak in tongues, they'd like to lay hands on the sick, but they aren't very eager to drink poison in front of other people.

Down south, however, I have seen this. I've seen people who literally took up snakes, and they believe they're fulfilling God's Word. Still, very few people did it. I've seen some with a snake saying "See!", and people praising the Lord, but there were very few volunteers. And as you know, many of those people have been bitten, and been very seriously ill, and some have even died.

Paul did these things, and he wasn't hurt (Acts 28), however, so there is such a thing. Let's call it physical protection.

Then it says, *"they will lay hands on the sick and they will recover"*. We already have healing, so we won't add that to our list.

"So you shall speak to all who are gifted artisans (craftsmen), whom I have filled with the spirit of wisdom, that they may make Aaron's garments, to sanctify him, that he may minister to Me as priest" (Exodus 28:3).

Then the Lord spoke to Moses, saying: "See, I have called by name Bezaleel the son of Uri, the son of Hur, of the tribe of Judah. And I have filled him with the Spirit of God, in wisdom, in understanding, in

knowledge, and in all manner of workmanship (craftmanship), to design artistic works, to work in gold, in silver, in bronze, in cutting jewels for setting, in carving wood, and to work in all manner of workmanship (craftsmanship). And I, indeed I, have appointed with him Aholiab the son of Ahisamach, of the tribe of Dan; and I have put wisdom in the hearts of all who are gifted artisans (craftsmen), that they may make all that I have commanded you" (Exodus 31:1).

This is language of the New Testament — *"being filled with the Spirit"*!

"And Bezaleel and Aholiab, and every gifted artisan in whom the Lord has put wisdom and understanding, to know how to do all manner of work for the service of the sanctuary, shall do according to all that the Lord has commanded." Then Moses called Bezaleel and Aholiab, and every gifted artisan in whose heart the Lord had put wisdom, everyone whose heart was stirred, to come and do the work" (Exodus 36:1-2).

The Holy Spirit uniquely equipped certain people at this time to do craftsmanship that was better than the average person could do. We do know that the work on this tabernacle (and eventually on the temple) was some of the most beautiful artwork ever known to man. This ability appears to have come specially from the Holy Spirit. So some people add the Gift of Craftmanship (gift twenty-seven) to their list.

But the Spirit of the Lord departed from Saul, and a distressing spirit from the Lord troubled him. And Saul's servant said to him, "Surely, a distressing spirit from God is troubling you. Let our master now command your servants, who are before you, to seek out a man who is a skillful player on the harp; and it shall be that he will play it with his hand when the distressing spirit from God is upon you, and you shall be well." So Saul said to his servants, "Provide me now a man who can play well, and bring him to me." Then one of the servants answered and said, "Look, I have seen a son of Jesse the Bethlehemite, who is skillful in playing, a mighty man of valor, a man of war, prudent in speech, and a handsome person; and the Lord is with him". And so it was, whenever the spirit from God was upon Saul, that David would take a harp and play it with his hand. Then Saul would become refreshed and well, and the distressing spirit would depart from him (I Samuel 16:14-18, 23).

Then, we must list the gift of music as gift twenty-eight. Now, we have twenty-eight gifts, and that's all I know that are listed in the Bible. Because the Spiritual Gifts are given by the Holy Spirit to the church, I have chosen not to add the Old Testament gifts of Craftsmanship and Music to our study. Also, we must acknowledge that some of the Gifts overlap in terms of our understanding and use.

THE PURPOSE OF SPIRITUAL GIFTS

SPECIAL GIFTS

Apostles
Prophets
Evangelists
Pastor/Teachers

• • • • • • • • • • • • • to EQUIP God's People

SPEAKING GIFTS

to EXPLAIN God's Truth • • • • • • • • • • •

Prophecy
Teaching
Exhortation
Word of Wisdom
Word of Knowledge

SERVING GIFTS

Leadership
Administration
Ministering
Showing Mercy
Faith
Discernment

• • • • • • • • • • • • • • • • • • to ENABLE God's Work

SUPPORT GIFTS

to ENABLE God's People • • • • • • • • • • • • • • • •

Helps
Giving
Hospitality

SIGN GIFTS

Miracles
Healings
Tongues
Interpretation
of Tongues

• • • • • • • • • • to ESTABLISH God's Authority

SPECIAL GIFTS

One of the crowning purposes of spiritual gifts surprises most people because we often think (rightly so) of the ministry of gifts as being between believers. Still, the ultimate purpose of gifts is evangelism. It is also the ultimate purpose of Christ and of His church. We can conclude that ultimately God has given His gifts for evangelism.

The Holy Spirit Himself has been given so that we would be saved. That is the point of the "initial gift". We are baptized with the Holy Spirit to be made members of the body of Christ. The Bible teaches that the baptism of the Holy Spirit is the means whereby we are made a part of the family of God.

We've seen that through the ministry of the Holy Spirit in the lives of believers, we are brought to maturity at which time we are enabled to "reproduce"; that is, we can bring others to Jesus Christ. The gift of the Spirit is for evangelism so that people will become Christians. We teach them God's Word and then when they repent, they receive everlasting life.

God's gifted men have different names and functions. They are called Apostles, Prophets, Evangelists, and Pastor-Teachers. Each one has a unique function in God's plan and the Bible words used for them help us to understand the differences and the importance that God places on them.

APOSTLE	PROPHET
Apostole is used 4 times	Propheteuo is used 29 times
Apostello is used 133 times	Prophetis and Propheteia each used 2 times
Apostolos is used 81 times	Prophetes is used 149 times

EVANGELIST	PASTOR/TEACHER
Euaggelistes is used 3 times	Poimen is used 18 times
Euaggelion is used 76 times	Poimaino is used 12 times
Euaggelidzo is used 51 times	Poimne and Poimnion each used 5 times
	Didaskalos is used 75 times
	Didasko is used 97 times
	Didaskalia is used 21 times
	Didache is used 30 times
	Didaktos is used 3 times
	Didaktikos 2 times

Special Gifts

There are gifts that are especially designed for the purpose of evangelism to lead people to Jesus Christ as Savior and Lord. These gifts are the gifted men Christ gave to His church.

And He Himself gave some to be apostles, some prophets, some evangelists, and some pastors and teachers (Eph. 4:11).

Two kinds of gifted men were especially designed for evangelism. First are apostles; second evangelists.

Apostles

I want to walk softly here on the subject of apostles, and yet I want to be open and honest with the information that's in the New Testament. If somebody asks me the question, "Are there apostles and prophets today?", I must answer "No" in the sense of writing Scripture. In the sense of laying the foundation of the church, the answer again is, "No". I disagree with certain cultic teachings which argue that we have apostles and prophets today.

Two young fellows stopped by my home, and their opening remark was, "Do you have apostles and prophets in your church?" In order to get a conversation going, I said "Yes". They were thrilled and said "Hey, great!" I said, "We hear from them each Sunday". They said, "That's remarkable! We can't believe it! Every week you hear from them?" I said, " Yes, every single week in our church we hear from the apostles and prophets. We hear from John, we hear from Paul......"

Yet when you put the Greek word "apostello" into Latin, you come up with a word that in English comes out *"missionary"*. The word *"missionary"* comes from a word which means *"to send from"*, assuming we send **from** someone, **to** someone. Is it possible that God could have people with an apostolic gift who do not write Scripture and are not a part of the Original Twelve, but they have a missionary gift? I think it's possible. It explains Timothy and Titus and Barnabas and several others, all of whom are called apostles. These men were running around with the apostle Paul all over the Roman empire. They were planting churches. They were introducing new communities to the gospel of Christ. If we understand their ministry as a missionary ministry, then maybe we have more apostles than we thought.

And so, I have made it my aim to preach the gospel, not where Christ was named, lest I should build on another man's foundation. (Rom. 15:20).

Paul said this of his own apostleship. God gave spiritual gifts (including gifted men) to Christ's church for evangelism—to preach the gospel. Characteristic of an apostle is a pioneering spirit, going to people who have not heard. The apostles' major ministry thrust was to evangelize. That was their first duty.

Barnabas was an apostle. It says the multitude of the city was divided, part sided with the Jews and part with the apostles (plural), meaning Paul and Barnabas.

When they had preached the gospel to that city and made many disciples, they returned to Lystra, Iconium and Antioch, strengthening the souls of the disciples, exhorting them to continue in the faith, and saying, "We must through many tribulations enter the kingdom of God." So when they had appointed elders in every church, and prayed with fasting, they commended them to the Lord in whom they had believed (Acts 14:21-23).

Then after some days Paul said to Barnabas, "Let us now go back and visit our brethren in every city where we have preached the word of the Lord, and see how they are doing" (Acts. 15:36).

So the work of an apostle is to preach the gospel, get involved in discipleship, teaching many, stengthening them to the point that they don't need to lean on him any more. He selects leadership, develops it, turns the work over to them and leaves town. He may come back and visit them, but he gets it going and takes off. That's an apostle. He has a pioneering spirit. He wants to preach Christ where He's never been named before.

God gave gifts to His church. In Ephesians 4, He gave Apostles, Prophets, Evangelists, Pastor-teachers. I don't read of any break between those four. He gave them all to God's church. It is very possible that today's apostles are simply our missionaries, pioneering in many cultures, telling people about the Lord, and introducing people to Jesus Christ. God bless them and may He increase their number.

Evangelists

It's very difficult to discuss the word *"evangelist"*. As a noun, it only appears three times in the entire New Testament (Eph. 4:11, Acts 21:8 and II Tim. 4:5).

Philip was one of the seven men chosen to distribute funds to widows, but he becomes a great sharer and preacher of the gospel. Acts 8 tells how he went to Samaria and introduced many people to the Lord. A great revival broke out there as multitudes came

to the Lord. He went to the desert and talked to one Ethiopian eunuch, reaching him with the gospel, preaching Jesus to him. Philip is found in all the cities of the Plain of Sharon sharing the gospel in all those cities. He went to Caesarea and possibly stayed there while his children were growing up. In Acts 21:8, he is called *"Philip the evangelist"*. He is the only man in the New Testament called *"the evangelist"*.

Timothy was also an apostle. The Apostle Paul wrote to him concerning his ministry over the churches, and he said, *"Do the work of an evangelist"*.

There are gifted people whom God has equipped, who are especially gifted in the area of evangelism. They have ease and effectiveness, and great joy in leading people to Christ. All of us are responsible to share the good news, but some of us have been equipped by the Holy Spirit to share the good news with great freedom and great effectiveness. These are *"evangelists"*.

God equips *"apostles"* with the leadership necessary not only to win people to Christ, but also to disciple and develop leaders to whom they can turn over the work, leave town and still have it remain.

The gift of the Holy Spirit is to bring people to Christ. The gifted men involved in evangelism are apostles and evangelists.

Are these professional ministers? God has given all of us gifts to use. There may be a lot of "laymen" who also have the gift of an apostle or an evangelist. Maybe God wants you to pick up from where you are and move to some other culture to tell folks in some other place about Jesus.

> *"And He Himself gave some to be apostles, some prophets, some evangelists, and some pastors and teachers, for the equipping of the saints (all believers) for the work of ministry (the use of spiritual gifts), for the edifying (or building up) of the body of Christ (Eph. 4:11-12).*

<u>THE CHURCH</u>
<u>WHICH IS HIS BODY</u>

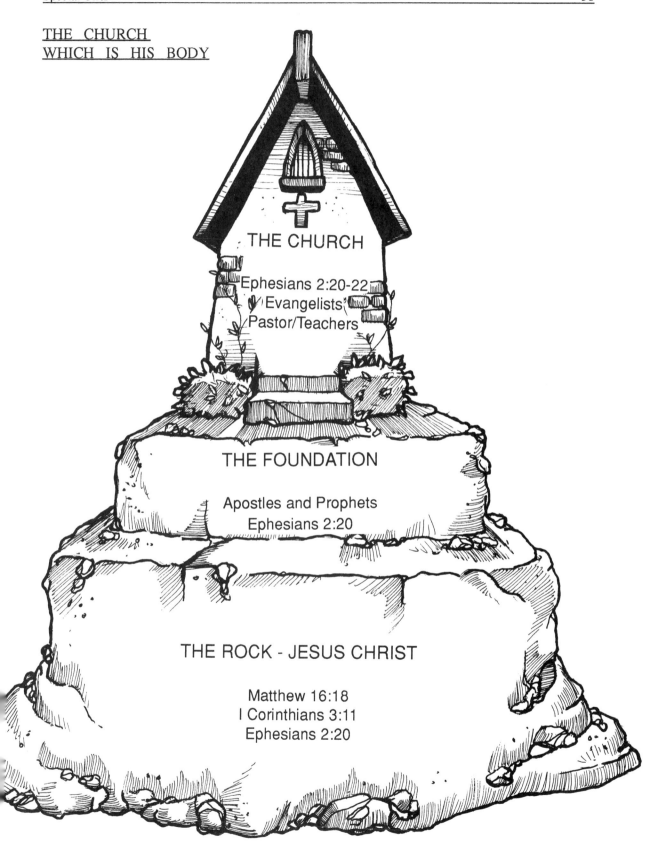

THE CHURCH

Ephesians 2:20-22
Evangelists
Pastor/Teachers

THE FOUNDATION

Apostles and Prophets
Ephesians 2:20

THE ROCK - JESUS CHRIST

Matthew 16:18
I Corinthians 3:11
Ephesians 2:20

GIFTS FROM JESUS CHRIST

The Head of the Church

APOSTLES   PROPHETS   EVANGELISTS   PASTOR/TEACHERS

SPECIAL GIFTS IN THE NEW TESTAMENT

APOSTLES

Acts 1:13, 26:	Peter	John	James
	Andrew	Philip	Thomas
	Bartholonew	Matthew	James (Alphaeus)
	Simon (Zealot)	Judas (James)	Matthias
Gal. 1:1	Paul		
I Thess. 1:1 cf.2:6	Barnabas	Timothy	
Rom. 16:7	Andronicus	Junias	
Phil. 2:25	Epaphroditus		
II Cor. 8:23	Titus		
Gal. 1:19	James (the Lord's brother)		

PROPHETS

Acts 11:27-28	Agabus	
Acts 15:32	Judas	Silas
Acts 13:1	Church of Antioch	
I Cor. 14:29	Church of Corinth	

EVANGELISTS

Acts 21:8	Philip

PASTOR-TEACHERS (Elders or Bishops)

I Peter 5:1	Peter
Acts 13:1	Church of Antioch
I Cor. 12:28	Church of Corinth
Acts 14:23	In every church
Titus 1:5	In every city
Acts 15:4, 23	Church of Jerusalem
Acts 20:17, 28	Church of Ephesus
Phil. 1:1	Church of Philippi
II Jn. 1, III Jn. 1	John

APOSTLES AND PROPHETS

The FOUNDATION of the Church   Ephesians 2:20

The REVELATION about the Church   Ephesians 3:5

The CONFIRMATION of the Word   Mark 16:17-20,
                                    Hebrews 2:3-4

THE FOUNDATION

Many Bible teachers believe that we no longer have apostles and prophets. We certainly have writings of those who penned Scripture. However, these teachers believe that the Gift of Apostle and the Gift of Prophet are not here today. Their reason is found in the Bible.

> ... having been built on the foundation of the apostles and prophets, Jesus Christ Himself being the chief cornerstone, in whom the whole building, being joined together, grows into a holy temple in the Lord, in whom you also are being built together for a habitation of God in the Spirit (Eph. 2:20).

Here the church is described as a building, and the foundation is described as being the apostles and prophets. You will often read or hear from Bible-teaching pastors and teachers that we are not building the foundation anymore. We're about ready to put the roof on. The Lord Jesus is coming soon, so to maintain the structural illustration, it would be impossible to argue for a continuing foundational ministry for the apostles and prophets.

THE REVELATION

> For this reason I, Paul, the prisoner of Jesus Christ for you Gentiles - if indeed you have heard of the dispensation of the grace of God which was given to me for you, how that by revelation He made known to me the mystery ....

The mystery he is talking about concerns the church and specifically the fact that Gentiles and Jews would be in the same body.

> ... He made known to me the mystery (as I wrote before in a few words, by which, when you read, you may understand my knowledge in the mystery of Christ), which in other ages was not made known to the sons of men (Old Testament times), as it has now been revealed by the Spirit to His holy apostles and prophets (Eph. 3:1-5)

The reason we don't have apostles and prophets (at least in the sense of their being the foundation of the church) is that he's talking about apostles and prophets who wrote Scripture—those men to whom the communication of New Testament truth was given. It

refers to the revelation that Paul says he got (now in the New Testament), and that which was received by all the apostles and prophets.

It's interesting that both of these passages (Ephesians 2:20 and 3:5) use the words *"apostles and prophets"*. That phrase is very common in Greek and is used to indicate that it connects equals. When two nouns are connected by *"and"* with the definite article in front of the first noun but not the second, it is connnecting equals. The text says *"the apostles and prophets"*. That means that the apostle being discussed is also a prophet.

According to the Bible, prophets wrote Scripture. People often say to me, prophets wrote in the Old Testament, apostles wrote in the New Testament. All of God's truth was communicated to writing prophets. The apostles were also prophets (according to these two verses) to whom God communicated truth that we now have in written form.

It also appears these apostles and prophets are a select group. It says He has revealed this *"by the Spirit to His holy apostles and prophets"*. That doesn't mean some apostles were unholy. The word *"holy"* means *"to set apart or to separate"*. He's saying there is a unique group of apostles and prophets who were set apart to receive direct revelation from God, and they wrote the Scripture which is the foundation for the church—namely, the New Testament.

If we believe that the apostles and prophets are those who wrote Scripture, then there are no apostles and prophets today. I believe that the Bible is very clear about its finality and completeness. Revelation 22 says that you can't "add to" it or "take away from" it. The Bible is a complete and final revelation. Jude 3 says it was *"once for all delivered to the saints"*. I take that to mean that it is a final message.

> God, who at various times and in different ways spoke *in time past* to the fathers by the prophets, has in these last days spoken to us (literally "in the last of these days"), by his Son (Heb. 1:1- 2).

There's an indication of the finality of God's direct revelation. God is no longer saying from the heavens, "David, can I have your attention, please? Now write down the following ...." He's not doing that anymore although a lot of people claim to be hearing it. God is not speaking audibly anymore.

It is necessary to argue that He IS still speaking in order to establish the basis of any false religion or cult! They claim to have writings that are equal to Scripture. They claim that God spoke to them. However, if they mean that apostles and prophets are still writing Scripture, receiving direct revelation from God, then scratch them off your list. There are no longer that kind of apostles and prophets.

Even after saying all this, I still want to put a question mark behind it. First of all, Barnabas was an apostle and he didn't write any Scripture. Timothy and Titus were apostles and they didn't write any Scripture. Silvanus was an apostle and he didn't write

any Scripture.   Epaphroditus was an apostle and he didn't write any Scripture. Andronicus and Junias were apostles and they didn't write any Scripture. Even in that day there were apostles who never wrote any Scripture.

Also on the other hand, the kind of apostles who were running around the Roman world planting churches are still here today! It wasn't until this century that we stopped calling missionaries "apostles". We stopped because we thought they were getting a little too authoritative; however, the word "apostle" put into Latin and then into English is our word "missionary".

Either the evangelist is the gifted person who is the missionary, or it's the apostle who is the missionary. If we have teachers today, why not prophets? A prophet does not simply predict the future. He is to speak before a crowd, in a public manner, and we have to rule them out because of Ephesians 2:20 and 3:5. So, I'm going to cross apostles and prophets off my list of gifts and thus stand in the main stream of Bible teachers through all the ages who do not believe we now have apostles and prophets.

Still, I'm not going to lean too far over there. I'm going to step a little to the right and say it's **possible** that we have some apostles and prophets today, but I'm not sure. At least we must take them off our list of gifts in the sense of writing Scripture, but how much further we eliminate them, I'm not really sure.

I hope this series on Spiritual Gifts will get us all to be careful in dealing with them. Let's look at the Scripture, let's examine the facts, and really see for ourselves. I'm not trying to cause debates, but I am trying to get us to be careful in communicating what the Scriptures teach. Don't be dogmatic that you've got the right answer and the right view-point. Good men have disagreed on this subject for years!

THE CONFIRMATION

How shall we escape if we neglect so great a salvation, which at the first begin to be spoken by the Lord, and was confirmed to us by those who heard Him, God also bearing witness both with signs and wonders, with various miracles, and gifts of the Holy Spirit, according to His own will (Heb. 2:3-4).

The little phrase *"signs and wonders, with various miracles"* appears often in the book of Acts.

Truly the signs of an apostle were accomplished among you with all perseverance, in signs and wonders and mighty deeds (II Cor. 12:12).

"These signs will follow those who believe: In My name they will cast out demons; they will speak with new tongues; they will take up serpents; and if they drink anything deadly, it will by no means hurt them; they will lay hands on the sick, and they will recover" (Mark 16:17-18).

Our Lord Jesus referred to these things as *"gifts"* which are *"signs"*. He said the same thing we found in Hebrews—these signs were to confirm the Word.

The word *"follow"* does not mean that the signs are done by the one who believes even though a certain group of churches argues that all believers will do these Sign Gifts. That is not what the text says. The word *"follow"* is our word *"accompany"* or *"alongside"*. The presence of the apostles would have been necessary because verse 20 says that the apostles *"went out and preached everywhere, the Lord working with them and confirming the word through the accompanying signs"*.

The proper way to say this would be that Jesus predicted that signs would be present when His apostles were giving out His message. Those who believed understood that the message was from God by the evidence of the signs. That's very important when it comes to believing New Testament truth.

Before the New Testament, all they had was the Old Testament. How were they to know that what the apostles were saying was Scripture and they should obey it? God's answer was to confirm the Word with miraculous signs.

Jesus names the gifts: *"casting out demons, speaking with new tongues, taking up serpents, drinking deadly things without being hurt, laying hands on the sick, and they recover."* These are the sign gifts. In Acts, casting out demons is called *"a miracle"* and uses the exact same word used in Mark. The same is true in the Gospels. Taking up serpents and drinking anything deadly are also called *"miracles"* as well as *"signs"* in the book of Acts.

Healings and miracles are here—plus tongues and interpretation of tongues. Out of our list of twenty-eight spiritual gifts, at least four would be called Sign Gifts — healings, miracles, tongues and interpretation of tongues. Those are the Sign Gifts.

It's clear that Sign Gifts are the confirmation of the apostles and their message. That was a revelation from God announcing that the gospel was to go to both Jews and Gentiles. That they would be in one body, the church, was a *"mystery"*. It was a brand new doctrine.

Tongues were the confirmation that their message was to Israel. Tongues were a sign of judgment to come. God would remove His blessing from unbelieving Israel and pour out His judgment against them. This is exactly what happened in 70 A.D. which is a full explanation for the absence of tongues in church history following that time.

QUALIFICATIONS OF LOCAL CHURCH LEADERS

Bishop/Elder
I Tim. 3:1-7,
Tit. 1:5-9

Deacon
Acts 6:3,
I Tim. 3:8-13

Deaconess
Rom. 16:2,
I Tim. 3:11

General Observations

Qualifications are not based on spiritual gifts.

Qualifications emphasize character and reputation more than ability and skill; that is, what a man is, is more important than what he can do.

God puts a continual desire for the office in the heart of the individual

If a man desires the position of a bishop, he desires a good work (I Tim. 3:1).

OREGO—to reach out after (present tense/middle voice).

EPITHUMEO—to fix the passion on a thing (present tense/active voice).

The qualifications should be recognized and agreed upon by the local church (Acts. 6:3, 5; 14:23; Titus 1:5).

RELATIONSHIPS AND DIFFERENCES BETWEEN GIFTS AND OFFICES

Apostles can be elders
I Peter 1:1 cf. 5:1; II John 1; III John 1
 Acts 5:12 - Granville Sharp's rule is that two nouns connected by "and" are equals when the definite article is in front of the first noun but not the second.

Apostles can be teachers
II Timothy 1:11

Elders are appointed by Apostles
Acts 14:23; I Timothy 5:22; Titus 1:5

Apostles are recognized by Elders
I Timoty 4:14 cf. II Timothy 1:6

Apostles are recognized by Prophets and Teachers
Acts 13:1-3

Elders are to function as Bishops
Acts 20:17, 28

Elders are called to shepherd or pastor
I Peter 5:1-2

Evangelists could be identified as Elders or Deacons
Acts 6:5 cf. 21:8—the seven chosen in chapter 6 may be elders rather than deacons. Also cf. Acts 11:30 and Acts 15:2.

It is possible to have Elders and Deacons who are not any of the four gifted men of Ephesians 4:11 and I Timothy 5:17.

Gifts	Offices
Apostles	Bishops/Elders
Prophets	Deacons
Evangelists	
Pastor/Teachers	

Speaking Gifts

The Gift of Prophecy/Preaching
The Gift of Wisdom
The Gift of Knowledge
The Gift of Teaching
The Gift of Counselling

There are five Speaking Gifts, but the first three do NOT deal with any additional understanding or knowledge from God. If our understanding is going to be that these gifts are to give brand new knowledge to the body of Christ, then I check out right there. The revelation of God is complete in the Old and New Testaments that we already have. I don't believe these gifts are to be understood in that sense.

The Gift of Prophecy

Some people have a problem with the Gift of Prophecy because they immediately identify this gift with predicting the future—giving some new revelation. However, the Gift of Prophecy is not simply to predict the future. It comes from two Greek words which mean *"to speak"* and *"beforehand"* or *"before"*. If we say *"beforehand"*, we refer to time and it means to predict the future; however, in New Testament times, it was used to apply to a person who spoke publicly— "before" people. Someone who proclaimed the message of the emperor in the town square (for instance) was a *"prophet"*.

Men with loud, foghorn-type voices were chosen for this job. That was necessary in the days before microphones. Whether they proclaimed a message that had been given to them or delivered a message about the future, the same word was used concerning them.

Technically, the restricted usage of the word *"prophet"* held strictly for predicting the future did not begin until the Middle Ages. In early times, it meant to speak forth what God had given to you. An example is Aaron, the High Priest, who is called *"the prophet of God"* in Exodus 7:1. He probably isn't on your list of Old Testament prophets. Why did God call him *"a prophet of God"*? Aaron never came up with any predictions.

Moses tried to excuse himself from obeying God's instructions by saying he wasn't eloquent. This wasn't true as we see from the things he wrote, but it was his excuse. God became angry and asked Moses who made his mouth. God's judgment was to send Aaron with him into the presence of Pharoah and Aaron did all the talking! My mind runs wild - Moses must have felt silly! After all, the Egyptians knew that he was well educated in all the training of the Egyptians. He walked in before Pharoah and Pharoah must have addressed Moses, "What do you want, Moses?" Then Moses punched Aaron and whispered into his ear, "Tell him to let my people go". Aaron bellowed, "Let my people go!" Pharoah must have looked at Moses and wondered what was wrong with this guy. I find it very amusing to think of Moses saying to Aaron, "Tell him this ...," "Tell him that." That was God's judgment on Moses. The interesting thing is that Aaron is called *"a prophet"* even though he never came up with anything on his own—he only said in Pharoah's court what Moses got from God and told him to say. Prophets are simply public speakers and whether they are prophets or not depends on whether or not their message came from God.

The prophets of the Old Testament said many things when they didn't have even the slightest understanding of what they were talking about. God said, "Say to the people thus and so" and they said them word for word. They said things about nations that hadn't even come into existence and a lot of other things they didn't understand at all. God just told them to speak forth what He said whether they understood or not.

In the New Testament, Christians prophesied—they spoke forth God's Word. Were they proclaiming the revelation that is now the New Testament or were they declaring God's Word after the New Testament was completed—using the Gift of Prophecy? I don't know. I have no idea. If you think that the Gift of Prophecy is proclaiming new revelation from God, however, I don't buy it. If you believe it is a spiritual gift of publicly communicating with large crowds, however, I can understand that.

I look at people like Billy Graham and I ask what his gift is and I think it's the ability to communicate with large crowds. I think the same about Luis Palau and others. This gift is to be used today in the context of what is already written. You can see two people stand before a large audience and one communicates and the other doesn't. How do you explain that? They may both be speaking forth God's Word, but people respond to the one and not the other.

The word *"prophet"* is used about 200 times in the Bible. In Romans 12, there is an interesting check on the Gift of Prophecy.

> *Having then gifts differing according to the grace that is given to us, let us use them. If prophecy, let us prophesy in proportion to our faith (Rom. 12:6).*

The word *"proportion"* is our word *"analogy"*, and in its basic form it means *"equality"* or *"agreement"*. Paul is saying that if you are going to preach (prophesy) make sure that it is equal with (or "in proportion to") your faith. That kind of faith is not your ability to believe. In Greek the definite article is in front of the word *"faith"*, so it is saying that preachers are to be sure their message is *"in agreement with"* THE faith. This is an absolute check on the preaching gift—you've got to preach the Word of God!

There are good public speakers who are not preaching the Word of God - that is not a spiritual gift. I've seen unbelievers who can really communicate in public but are not preaching the Bible. This gift is to proclaim the Bible in whatever setting the speaker finds himself and it has to be in agreement with the Word of God.

Word of Wisdom

I believe the same about this gift that I said about the Gift of Prophecy— if you say this is new revelation, I check out there. If you mean that it is communicating what is in the Scriptures, then I see the possibilities just as I do in preaching and teaching. In speaking gifts, all are to communicate God's Word. That's the check on these gifts.

To one is given the word of wisdom through the Spirit. To another the word of knowledge through the same Spirit (I Cor. 12:8).

These are speaking gifts—they are called "WORD of Wisdom" and "WORD of Knowledge". This is not talking about someone who sits in the pew with a lot of knowledge and never says anything. This gift is the ability to speak forth the wisdom and knowledge.

Also, the *"word"* is singular in both cases. It appears to refer to a particular instance or situation in which knowledge is used. Some say this indicates the infrequent use of these gifts. The speaker is not necessarily wiser than anybody else—he has the same Book to study that the rest of us have. However, he has ability to express that wisdom in a particular situation which is not given to everyone else even though we all may know it. God may use his words to communicate His will to a group to resolve a difficulty.

Solomon is the great example in I Kings 3. In a very wise way, he dealt with the problem of the two harlots who claimed the same baby. He had a Word of Wisdom. In the New Testament, wisdom is mentioned 75 times. What is wisdom? In the Old Testament, the word used emphasizes skill rather than knowledge. The very word is *"the ability to do something"*. In the New Testament, the Greek word is *"sophia"* from which we get that beautiful woman's name. It is the ability, not obvious to the average person, to have insight into people and situations. This is combined with knowing what to do and how to do it.

Word of Knowledge

This must be the most difficult gift to have and try to tell someone that you have it. There is a great danger in being arrogant if you have this gift. The Bible says, *"Knowledge puffs up"*, and it does.

Again, the use of the singular here indicates a particular situation where knowledge is needed. Knowledge is the observation of a lot of facts. These people are not "shoot from the hip" kind of people. Sometimes this kind of person can bore you to death because they are so thorough that they don't come up with quick answers. This is the kind of person who prepares lexicons and other study tools which the rest of us use. They don't usually care much for people, but this gift is the ability to communicate the observation on which the study is given. We need people like that.

The Gift of Teaching

There is a check in Romans 12 on teaching also. It mentions prophecy and ministry (service), then it says, "... *and he who teaches in teaching.*" The word for teaching most commonly used in the New Testament has various forms which give additional meaning. One form may mean *"the act of teaching"* while another would mean *"the teacher himself"*. Other forms of the word would mean *"the result of teaching,"* and *"the content of what is taught"*.

In this verse, *"he who teaches"* refers to the act of teaching, but the qualification is *"in teaching"* and that refers to the content of what is taught. Once again, the teaching is the Word of God. The act of teaching is not to teach biology. The Gift of Teaching cannot apply to secular subjects. The spiritual gift of teaching is relegated to teaching God's Word. I have found people who are not well trained yet have a beautiful ability to teach God's Word. This gift is not dependent on secular education. I'd like to unlock all those who have the Gift of Teaching so that they weren't held back by their lack of training and/or education.

These teachers don't care about the crowd. Preacher-types care, but teachers don't care if five or five hundred are listening. They just love to teach. These teachers are not public speakers for large crowds. Their great joy is in communicating God's Word.

There are all kinds of teaching. Don't be too restrictive when you look at spiritual gifts. God ministers them in a variety of ways. Some people think you can't really teach unless you can teach adults. There is a variety of the ways in which the Gift of Teaching is used. We don't need to use our gift the same way that others use their gift.

> *A servant of the Lord must not quarrel, but be gentle to all, able to teach, patient, in humility correcting those who are in opposition, if God will perhaps grant them repentance, so that they will know the truth, and that they will come to their senses and escape the snare of the devil, having been taken captive by him to do his will (II Tim. 2:24).*

Now, we either have a very carnal believer here or an unbeliever. Is it possible that teaching could be used in evangelism?

"They ceased not to teach and preach Jesus Christ" is a phrase used over and over again in the Book of Acts. Teaching can be used in evangelism as well as in edifying believers. In the area of evangelism, we need teachers. Paul had a great ministry of teaching unbelievers that came to him, as well as teaching believers.

One of the great needs in the Body of Christ is for teachers to teach new converts in simple language.

> *Though by this time you ought to be teachers, you need someone to teach you again the first principles of the oracles of God. You have come to need milk and not solid food. Everyone who partakes only of milk is unskilled in the Word of righteousness, for he is a babe. But solid food belongs to those who are of full age, that is those who by reason of use have their senses exercised to discern both good and evil (Heb. 5: 12-14).*

Jesus said that we are to teach those that we disciple. We are to teach those whom we baptize. We are to teach them to observe all that He commanded us (see Matt. 28:20).

These things (if you make a list of them) are not all the teachings of the Bible but they are principles for new believers. This refers to prayer and loving one another and the other basic principles which we are to teach to new believers. There is a discipleship — a teaching ministry — that is desperately needed for new believers. We need those who will concentrate on new believers and will help them. I call this "spiritual pediatrics". We need this kind of teacher.

Another type of teacher is the pastor/teacher who equips the believer for ministry (Eph. 4). In II Tim. 4:2, Paul speaks of counselors who also teach. Sometimes when

people seek counseling, they need a counselor, but sometimes when they go for counseling, they need a teacher. We need to be careful here. There is a difference. The teacher probably will not be so good at comforting and giving strokes, so you had better be ready for them. They will be bored with your problems and will want you to get to the point and let them know what they can do about your situation. The counselor will be tender and sensitive and will love to hear all about your problems. They will understand and will have words of wisdom to offer you.

Sometimes, however, you need a teacher to give you answers which you can use in solving the problems you face. Other times, you need the comfort of a sympathetic ear. There is a variety of gifts within the body of Christ and instead of getting upset with one another, we need to recognize the differences. God has given us all kinds of ways to use these gifts — and it's wonderful.

A teacher will explain the Word of God, and too often we think that refers only to a pastor. Nonetheless, there are times when people who have the gift of teaching explain the Word of God to a preacher/type of person.

> *Now a certain Jew named Apollos, born at Alexandria, an eloquent man and mighty man in the Scriptures, came to Ephesus. This man had been instructed in the way of the Lord; and being fervent in spirit, he spoke and taught accurately the things of the Lord, though he knew only the baptism of John. So he began to speak boldly in the synagogue. When Aquila and Priscilla heard him, they took him aside and explained to him the way of God more accurately (Acts 18:24-26).*

Aquila and Priscilla were great lay people and in the next verses it tells us how Apollos *"vigorously refuted the Jews publicly, showing from the Scriptures that Jesus is the Christ."* He used the instruction these lay people had given him and he used it to good effect. What a wonderful thing it was for them to teach Apollos. They saw the hand of God on this preacher, and they saw that he didn't know everything he needed to know, so they took him aside and filled him in on the facts. They told him that the Messiah had come, and there was great excitement. Then, Apollos went out and preached the death and resurrection of the Messiah.

The Gift of Counselling

One of the great troubles
in the body of Christ is the
whole concept of professional
counselling. We ignore the
Gift of Counselling
that God has given
the body of Christ
and as a result,
we think if a man
has a title and a
shingle hanging out,
he is the only one
who can answer
our needs. We
can't all go to him.

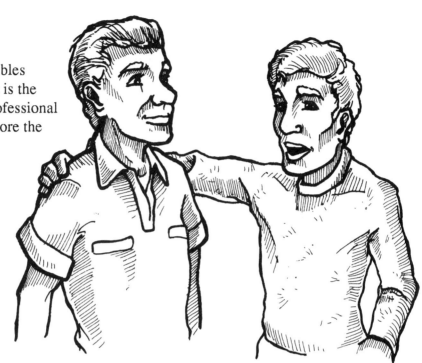

On the other hand, when we think a person who has not had professional training cannot counsel us, we are insulting the Holy Spirit. Some of the greatest counsel I have received has been from laymen who have the Gift of Counselling. I've also been to professional counsellors and I thank God for all of them. I especially thank God for a professional counsellor who also has the spiritual gift, for the best counselling comes from those who have the Gift of Counselling.

He who exhorts, in his exhortation ... (Rom. 12:8).

The first word *"exhort"* refers to the process and the second (*"exhortation"*) speaks of the content. Again, we see here the qualification that the counsel comes from the Scriptures (Rom. 15:4). The Scripture has all the comfort we need; however, some people understand the Scriptures but still don't have the ability to communicate it. That's the gift. Anyone who "counsels", or "exhorts", or "comforts" must stick to the content revealed in the Scripture about counsel.

The word *"counsel"* literally means *"one called alongside of"* and is translated with several words. If you have the Gift of Counsel, it is probably a one-on-one ministry.

Scripture deals more with what happened than with why it happened. In secular counselling, there is a great emphasis on **why** things happened. They look into a person's childhood and they look at the relationship with parents on the basis that once you know what happened, you will be able to resolve the problem. I happen to believe that it is impossible to really know why we did what we did. But just suppose we could come to know why, would it really solve the problem? I don't think so. Sometimes people leave the counsellor's office and do the same thing again.

In biblical counselling, counsellors deal with **what** has happened and what can be done about it. They don't simply want to know why something happened.

In ancient times, the counsellor was a legal advisor. Sometimes that is true today. In I John 2:2 we find the word *"advocate"* for counsellor because Jesus is a defense attorney. True counsel refers to legal advice. In the Bible, counselling either advises people to do something (explaining how it can be done) or it counsels people about what has already happened, and helps them (emotionally) to live with the situation.

Barnabas was called *"the son of counsel"* or encouragement. Many people should be getting involved in the lives of other people and using the gift of counselling which God has given us.

Four Ways of Counselling

> *As you know how we exhorted, and comforted, and charged every one of you, as a father does his own children (I Thess. 2:11).*

There are four ways in which Bible counselling takes place. The first is *"as a father..."* would counsel his children.

> *Now we exhort you, brethren, warn those who are unruly, comfort the fainthearted, uphold the weak, be patient with all (I Thess. 5:14).*

We see the second way in the last phrase of this verse. We aren't counselling in a biblical manner until we do it with **patience**. One of the keys to knowing that you do NOT have the gift of counselling is that you are impatient with someone who comes to you wanting to share his burden. If you are impatient with him, you are manifesting the opposite of what the Bible teaches.

When you look at verse 14, you are to do what it says,

> *"Warn the unruly"*; don't "Warn the fainthearted".

> *"Comfort the fainthearted"*; don't "Comfort the unruly".

Don't mix up those things.

However, no matter what people's needs are, we are to be patient.

The third way that Bible counselling takes place is in conjunction with teaching.

> Preach the Word! Be ready in season and out of season. Convince, rebuke, exhort (counsel), with all longsuffering (patience) and teaching (II Tim. 4:2).

It is NOT biblical counselling when there is no teaching from God's Word. The counsel that God is talking about is the counsel of His Word. If there is no instruction, no teaching of the Scriptures, there is no biblical counselling.

One final way in which we are to counsel is with authority.

> Speak these things, exhort (counsel), and rebuke with all authority (Tit. 2:15).

We are not to back down if the Scripture is clear on the matter under discussion. I've found that those who don't have the gift of counselling find it difficult to *"convince"*, to *"rebuke"* and to *"confront"*. Some people mix the Gift of Showing Mercy with the Gift of Counselling because it is sensitive and comforting. Sometimes the Gift of Counselling **confronts** the person seeking counsel. Counselling sometimes **rebukes** the person, making it clear that there must be a change; things must be different. Many who don't have the Gift of Counselling get weak knees at that point and don't have the authority that goes with this gift.

The person who can't rebuke a person, as well as comforting and teaching, is not a counsellor. This gift carries with it the ability to confront on the basis of God's Word when that is what's needed.

SERVING GIFTS

Gifts of Leadership

Most of the books on this subject deal with
Exodus 18 because Moses is the first
example of leadership in the Bible. We can
see from this passage why we need leadership in
the body of Christ.

There aren't very many people who want to be leaders today. The credibility gap is one of the reasons for this. A lot of leaders have failed us. Another reason is that people have seen what others do to leaders. When you are visible, you have to be ready for the "pot shots". People don't seem to mind doing this to a leader even though they would never treat a friend that way. Some people even call this "the price of leadership". Another reason people hesitate to take leadership is the price of loneliness. The more you lead, the less you can enjoy the fellowship of God's people. You suddenly become "wierd" to them and they don't want to be close.

People have all kinds of attitudes toward leaders and it has created a "crisis in leadership". We have a real need to restore the biblical concepts of leadership. God has given gifts to His people and one of the gifts is leadership.

The Need For Leadership

And so it was, on the next day, that Moses sat to judge the people; and the people stood before Moses from morning until evening. So when Moses' father-in-law saw all that he did for the people, he said, "What is this thing that you are doing for the people? Why do you alone sit, and all the people stand before you from morning until evening?" And Moses said to his father-in-law, "Because the people come to me to inquire of God. When they have a difficulty, they come to me, and I judge between one and another; and I make known the statutes of God and His laws."

So Moses' father-in-law said to him, "The thing that you do is not good. Both you and these people who are with you will surely wear yourselves out. For this thing is too much for you; you are not able to perform it by yourself. Listen now to my voice; I will give you counsel, and God will be with you: Stand before God for the people, so that you may bring the difficulties to God. (In leadership, prayer comes first.) And you shall teach them the statutes and the laws, and show them the way in which they must walk and the work they must do. (Teaching comes next in leadership.)

Moreover you shall select from all the people able men, such as fear God, men of truth, hating covetousness; and place such over them to be rulers of thousands, rulers of hundreds, rulers of fifties, and rulers of tens. And let them judge the people at all times. Then it will be that every great matter they shall bring to you, but every small matter they themselves shall judge. So it will be easier for you, for they will bear the burden with you.

So they judged the people at all times; the 'hard' cases they brought to Moses, but they judged every small case themselves. Then Moses let his father-in-law depart, and he went his way to his own land (Ex. 18:13-27).

The basic qualification for leadership is a godly lifestyle. There are unbelievers and carnal Christians who are leaders, but we are talking here about spiritual leadership. That requires a godly lifestyle.

I wonder if Jethro was telling Moses that the rulers could handle things *"at all times"* and that **there wouldn't be** any *"great matters"* for him to judge. I'm just drawing this from what is said, but it seems like that to me.

The basic unit here is ten. This guides my thinking to consider that if there are more than ten people who report directly to you, we will soon see "the Moses syndrome". We have to develop a concept where more people are leaders.

The need for leadership in the body of Christ is tremendous. You either have a leader by choice or by default. We need leaders in every group. The chairman is not always the leader. Authority comes by the Gift of Leadership, not by appointment or by election of the people.

The Gift of Leadership

Some books on this subject name only one gift here, but the Holy Spirit used two words for this and, therefore, we need to understand that there are two gifts. The word in Romans 8 is not the same as the word used in I Corinthians 12.

... he who leads, with diligence ... (Rom. 12:8).

That same word *"leads"* is translated *"rule"* and *"manage"*. There are a lot of words we could use, but the Greek word literally means *"to stand before"*. It means to have charge over people, too, but it conveys the idea of motivating the group. It is used in the New Testament eight times. It is used of fathers, elders, bishops and deacons.

A Father Whose Children Submit to His Leadership

... one who rules his own house well, having his children in submission with all reverence (for if a man does not know how to rule his own house, how will he take care of the church of God?) (I Tim. 3:4-5).

"Reverence" here is a special word having to do with a seriousness of mind, especially about spiritual things. It doesn't mean that the father never has fun with his kids. It does indicate that when it comes to spiritual things, there is a certain seriousness about this dad and that makes it an important qualification for leadership in the church.

> *... if a man is blameless, the husband of one wife, having faithful children not accused of dissipation or insubordination (Tit. 1:6).*

This can mean that he has *"children of the faith"* (believers) or it can mean that the children are loyal and trustworthy. It could mean that they are loyal to their father and he can trust them. There are a lot of views.

The description of a leader here is of one who has things under control. The real measure of that is from the negative view — "Are the children rebellious? Do the children have respect for this man's leadership?" Sometimes we see what a man is by what he is not. Children can rebel because they have a sin nature, but when you want to know a man's habit of life, you ask the question, "Do his children respect his authority?"

When we look at the leaders in God's church, we see the importance of the submission of those who are to follow. If there is someone who claims to be a leader but people are unwilling to follow him, we have to question whether or not he has the Gift of Leadership.

It Involves Taking Care of People's Needs

> *... how will he **take care** of the church of God? (I Tim. 3:5).*

Sometimes our ideas of leadership come out of the secular world instead of from the Word of God. God's leaders are *"to take care of"* the people of God. The same word is found in the story of the Good Samaritan.

> *Then Jesus answered and said: " A certain man went down from Jerusalem to Jericho, and fell among thieves, who stripped him of his clothing, wounded him, and departed, leaving him half dead. Now by chance a certain priest came down that road. And when he saw him, he passed by on the other side. Likewise a Levite, when he arrived at the place, came and looked, and passed by on the other side. But a certain Samaritan, as he journeyed, came where he was. And when he saw him, he had compassion on him, and went to him and bandaged his wounds, pouring on oil and wine; and he set him on his own animal, brought him to an inn, **and took care of him"** (Luke 10:30-34).*

This is the same word here *("took care of him")* as we found in I Timothy 3 *("take care of the church of God")*. It happens again in the next verses:

> *"On the next day, when he departed, he took out two denarii, gave them to the innkeeper, and said to him, '**Take care of him;** and whatever more you spend, when I come again, I will repay you.' So which of these three do you think was neighbor to him who fell among the thieves?" (Luke 10:35-36).*

Leadership in the church means that people follow your example and you respond to the needs of people. We must be interested in the area of the gift that God gives us and we should see the proper response of people when we exercise that gift.

> *This is a faithful saying, and these things I want you to affirm constantly, that those who have believed in God should be careful to maintain (lead) [in the area of] good works (Titus 3:8).*

> *And let our people also learn to maintain (lead) good works, to meet urgent needs, that they may not be unfruitful (Tit. 3:14).*

When you break this down step by step, you can learn a great deal. The surest way to know that you are a leader is when you see your people become more productive. Secular leadership expects the people under their care to make them look good. That is NOT what God expects. Leadership doesn't always need to be seen. Their greatest joy is to see the people they are in charge of become productive in their lives.

Real Leadership Responds Quickly to Needs that Exist

Every time you find someone who wants to take care of a need right away, you have found a leader. They don't want to take their time; they want to do something about a problem or meet a need right away. They are full of ideas on how to meet the needs.

> *... he who leads, with diligence ... (Rom. 12:8).*

"Diligence" here is the word for *"haste"*. The leader wants to do things right away — speedily. Do it now! It doesn't mean that we don't communicate with people, or that we don't think things through. It doesn't mean that we give up the broad perspective on things. However, if you see things that are needed and you are frustrated by how long it takes to get them done, perhaps you have the Gift of Leadership. Some people sit in meetings and get thoroughly frustrated because of the lack of leadership. Guess what!

That person is the leader!

The other people in the meetings didn't even notice that things weren't getting accomplished.

Leaders see the problems and they want to respond quickly.

Leaders Work Best With Groups of People

We've talked about the word *"leader"* meaning someone who stands in front of people. These people get frustrated with one-on-one relationships. It takes too much time to go to people one at a time. A leader who wants to reach six people will gather them together and motivate all of them (more quickly and better) as a group. He isn't inclined to meet with each one individually. He wants to stand before the group.

The Gift of Administration

We hear it said, "Nobody likes an administrator." We often see these people as those who don't care much for people. They seem abrupt. This is in contrast to leaders who have a people orientation, but an administrator is a task-oriented person. Sometimes we get hurt by not understanding this and by forgetting that the body of Christ needs both kinds of leaders.

> *And God has appointed these in the church: first apostles, second prophets, third teachers, after that miracles, then gifts of healings, helps, administrations (governments) (I Cor. 12:28).*

What are *"administrations"* or *"governments"*? The Greek word means *"a helmsman"*. He was not the **owner** of the ship, but he was the one **in charge** of seeing that the vessel, its cargo and its passengers arrived safely in port. In Acts 27, a helmsman had to make a decision to throw some cargo overboard. He had to cut some of the supplies in order to save some lives. That's an administrator. He sometimes has to make some hard decisions. He has to cut back some places in order reach the overall goal. A lot of people don't like administrators because of that, but we need them.

The helmsman is mentioned in Ezekiel and in Revelation and is often translated *"shipmasters"*. The root word means *"to steer a ship"*. In the writings of Plato it meant someone who knew all the times of the sky, and knew the days of the year and the currents. Our modern word *"navigator"* would fit the administrator nicely. He is a guide who can steer the ship. People come with many needs, but we must get the ship safely into the harbor and for this, we need a navigator. That's why he has to make hard decisions.

1. A helmsman, an administrator is responsible for the direction of things. The church must know where it needs to go and why. These people are needed.
2. He needs to be able to make decisions quickly. When the cargo and the passengers are at stake, someone needs to make a decision quickly as how best to ensure their safety.
3. An administrator must sense deeply his accountability to God and not be swayed by the pressures of the people around him. This is important because (for the local church) the "ship owner" is God Himself. The helmsman was employed by the owner and given full charge for the safe delivery of the ship and the cargo. If he lost any of it, he was accountable to pay the owner back. He was the one who gave direction to the oarsmen and the crew of the ship in order to get them safely to their goal.
4. The helmsman must also respond quickly in time of storm. In Roman law, there is an indication that this man could pay with his life if he left the ship in time of storm. That's quite serious. That God would use this kind of man as an illustration of one of His spiritual gifts is amazing.

There are people who can stay with the ship even when it looks like there is serious trouble. This man has loyalty and is determined to steer the ship back on its course. He demonstrates a certain confidence that keeps others calm in a time of difficulty.

The problem is that people view these two gifts so differently. Real differences arise when they are not viewed separately. An administrator is scared to death to stand before the crowd and try to motivate them. He doesn't like that and he might get so nervous you might conclude he isn't even a leader. There are many people who work in leadership who are like this. They aren't visible and they don't **want** to be, but they are directing the course — calm, trusting God, making tough decisions when necessary.

Sometimes the administrator doesn't understand the leader, either. He's always motivating. These two on the same committee are interesting. The leader is getting everyone to see the vision of what can be done, while the administrator is asking, "How much will it cost?" He has his yellow pad and pencil out beginning to write down numbers. The leader responds with, "You're always talking about money!" Calmly, the administrator says, "Somebody has to." You'll never get agreement from these two.

We've all seen it in our church activities. What I want you to see is that God is a God of varieties. He has given a variety of gifts which can be used in a variety of ways to meet any number of needs in the body of Christ. Every snowflake is different. Every gift from God is different.

A Word of Caution

> *Remember those who rule over you (lead), who have spoken the word of God to you, whose faith follow, considering the outcome of their conduct (Heb. 13:7).*

Leadership here is not the word we looked at earlier, but a **general** word for leading. The great grief in the heart of God's people is the tragedies that happen in the lives of leaders. The Bible says we are to speak the Word of God; we're to be controlled by the Word of God. It is the faith and confidence in God's Word that is the example for others. People have a right to examine the outcome of their conduct. We should know what their lives are like because we actually lead by example, not by our words alone.

The Gift of Ministry

Everybody is to be serving in the body of Christ, but if you have the Gift of Ministry, you really need to be using it because it is desperately needed in the body of Christ.

> *Having then gifts differing according to the grace that is given to us, let us use them: if prophecy, let us prophesy in proportion to our faith; or ministry, let us use it in our ministering ... (Rom. 12:6).*

The English word *"deacon"* comes from the word *"minister"*. There are about 103 mentions of this word in the New Testament. We are to be ministers in some sense; we are all to be *"deacons"*. One of the root ideas included is *"to raise the dust by hastening"*. People who have this gift get on with the job at hand — they want to get things done.

The first usage of this word within the church was for the matter of distributing to the material needs of widows.

> *Now in those days, when the number of the disciples was multiplying, there arose a murmuring against the Hebrews by the Hellenists, because their widows were neglected in the daily distribution. Then the twelve summoned the multitude of the disciples and said, "It is not desirable that we should leave the word of God and serve tables (minister). Therefore, brethren, seek out from among you seven men of good reputation, full of the Holy Spirit and wisdom, whom we may appoint over this business (Acts 6:1-3).*

This shows that ministering has to do with the physical needs of widows — and presumably anyone in need. This is the most prominent usage of this word in the ancient world. It is used in the story of the marriage at Cana of Galilee.

> *His mother (Jesus' mother) said to the servants (deacons), "Whatever He says to you, do it" (John 2:5).*

According to this verse, the servants are called by the same word *"deacon"* that we are talking about here, and they were told to do whatever Jesus said for them to do.

> *When the master of the feast had tasted the water that was made wine, and did not know where it came from (but the servants who had drawn the water knew), the master of the feast called the bridegroom ... (John 2:9).*

These servants were waiting on the guests to meet their every need.

Martha was distracted with much serving (ministering), and she approached Him and said, "Lord, do You not care that my sister has left me to serve (minister) alone? Therefore tell her to help me." And Jesus answered and said to her, "Martha, Martha, you are worried and troubled about many things. But one thing is needed, and Mary has chosen that good part, which will not be taken away from her" (John 10:40-42).

There they made Him a supper; and Martha served (Jn. 12:2).

Lazarus was there, too. In Luke 10, Martha was **disturbed** about the work of serving. She wasn't using the gift that God gave her wisely. Her attitude was wrong and she was exercising her gift with carnality. But in John 12, there is no word of condemnation from Jesus and it is clear now that He had not intended that she stop serving. He wanted her to get her priorities straightened out, so Martha was again doing what she enjoyed doing.

In the body of Christ, we need servers and the basic idea of what deacons were in the early church was to wait tables. We're talking about waiters and waitresses. If that's what God calls you to do, there is **joy** in doing this. There are those who enjoy serving people.

The angels serve people. They even came to serve Jesus. They served Him food, and they served food to the Old Testament prophets. They are *"ministering spirits"* says Hebrews 1:14. One of the qualities of someone who has this gift is that they enjoy it.

Sometimes people think that serving is not as important as discipling someone and being involved in the lives of people. Don't confuse people who are doing this job by telling them they should be doing something else.

> *But thanks be to God who puts the same earnest care for you into the heart of Titus. For he not only accepted the exhortation, but being more diligent, he went to you of his own accord. And we have sent him the brother whose praise is in the gospel throughout all the churches, and not only that, but who was also chosen by the churches to travel with us with this gift, which is administered by us to the glory of the Lord Himself and to show your ready mind, avoiding this: that anyone should blame us in this lavish gift which is administered (served) by us (II Cor. 8:16-20).*

Here they are distributing to the needs of people and serving them. Our whole ministry of ushers is included here and God honors this service.

The Gift of Showing Mercy

... he who shows mercy,
with cheerfulness (Rom. 12:8).

This gift has to do with feeling sympathy and having compassion. Forms of the word appear about 60 times in the New Testament. It is used often of Jesus and God's mercy and salvation, as well as in regard to healing. I'd like you to understand this gift and the people in the body of Christ who have this gift which is most often found in connection with meeting the physical needs of people.

> *When Jesus departed from there, two blind men followed Him, crying out and saying, "Son of David, **have mercy on us!**" (Matt. 9:27).*

These men were blind and they wanted to see, so they called out to Jesus to have mercy on them.

> *And behold a woman of Canaan came from that region and cried out to Him, saying, "**Have mercy on me,** O Lord, Son of David! My daughter is severely demon-possessed" (Matt. 15:22).*

> *"Lord, **have mercy on my son,** for he is an epileptic and suffers severely; for he often falls into the fire and often into the water" (Matt. 17:15).*

Ths man is pleading for Jesus to understand what he is going through. How does this read into the Gift of Mercy?

> *And behold two blind men sitting by the road, when they heard that Jesus was passing by, cried out, saying, "**Have mercy on us,** O Lord, Son of David!" Then the multitude warned them that they should be quiet; but they cried out all the more, saying, "**Have mercy on us,** O Lord, Son of David!" So Jesus stood still and called them, and said, "What do you want Me to do for you?" They said to Him, "Lord, that our eyes may be opened." So Jesus had compassion **and** touched their eyes. And immediately their eyes received sight, and they followed Him (Matt. 20:30-34).*

Compassion is an essential quality in showing mercy. So, we see in the New Testament, that cry, *"Have mercy on me!"* is used very often in connection with this gift. Therefore, the Gift of Showing Mercy must contain the idea of having compassion on the sick and suffering. Still, I doubt that you have the Gift of Showing Mercy unless you want to be **involved** in someone's problem.

There is more to the gift than **just** showing mercy. Many of us feel compassion but don't have the gift of knowing how to act on those feelings.

Then Jesus answered and said: "A certain man went down from Jerusalem to Jericho, and fell among thieves, who stripped him of his clothing, wounded him, and departed, leaving him half dead. Now by chance a certain priest came down that road. And when he saw him, he passed by on the other side. Likewise a Levite, when he arrived at the place, came and looked, and passed by on the other side. But a certain Samaritan, as he journeyed, came where he was. And when he saw him, he had compassion on him, and went to him and bandaged his wounds, pouring on oil and wine; and he set him on his own animal, brought him to an inn, and took care of him. On the next day, when he departed, he took out two denarii, gave them to the inndeeper, and said to him, 'Take care of him; and whatever more you spend, when I come again, I will repay you.' So which of these three do you think was neighbor to him who fell among the thieves?" And he said, "He who showed mercy on him." Then Jesus said to him, "Go and do likewise" (Luke 10:30-37).

Samaritans today number only a small group of people. They live in two spots in Israel and the government gives them complete physical care. They only marry each other — brothers and sisters. As a result, there is a great deal of mental derangement and physical deformity. They are a pitiful people. But in this story, it was the Samaritan who had mercy on the man who fell among thieves.

All of us are required to show mercy, but there are some in the body of Christ who have the Gift of Showing Mercy which causes them to show mercy toward the sick and suffering. This is not just the feelings of compassion that cause us to stop and look, but the willingness to get involved in people's lives and do something about their problem.

At Joppa there was a certain disciple named Tabitha, which is translated Dorcas. This woman was full of good works and charitable deeds (showed mercy) which she did (Acts. 9:36).

The things she did give us insight into what it means to have mercy and to have the Gift of Showing Mercy. What she had been doing came to light after she died and Peter arrived.

Then Peter arose and went with them. When he had come, they brought him to the upper room. And all the widows stood by him weeping, showing the tunics and garments which Dorcas had made while she was with them (Acts. 9:39).

It appears that the Gift of Mercy has to do with clothes she provided for the widows who were needy. Often in Scripture, Paul wrote that the church should be careful of the widows who had been left out of society and had no family to support them. The church

was to support them and not leave them out in the cold. Dorcas was providing them clothes.

The Gift of Showing Mercy is DOING something about the needs of people. However, there is one little qualification. We think of sympathetic people often as being sad and somber, but Romans 12:8 says *"... with cheerfulness"*. The Greek word is with *"hilarity"*.

For instance, is that what we usually think of when we think of a hospital ministry? I think not. If you're the one who is sick, you know how valuable the cheerfulness is — *"a joyful readiness of mind"*. I think this is a great gift for hospital chaplains and others who like to do hospital visitation. How wonderful to cheer up the one who is suffering — this takes a willingness to become involved and to do something about the physical problems that people face.

The Gift of Faith

This gift is listed among nine in I Corinthians and is found in the midst of "the Gifts of Healings" and the Gift of Miracles. It cannot be saving faith because we all have that. I think the reference to this special Gift of Faith is found in the following passage:

> *And though I have the gift of prophecy, and understand all mysteries and all knowledge, and though I have all faith, so that I could remove mountains, but have not love, I am nothing (I Cor. 13:2).*

Here he is writing about gifts and showing how love is greater than the gifts. Then is not this the mention of the Gift of Faith? A lot of people don't recognize it as such, but the key is that it goes on to say *"... so that I could remove mountains"*. That's the Holy Spirit saying that the Gift of Faith is the ability to move mountains. Where in the Bible does it talk about *"moving mountains"*?

> *And when they had come to the multitude, a man came to Him, kneeling down to Him and saying, "Lord, have mercy on my son, for he is an epileptic and suffers severely; for he often falls into the fire and often into the water. So I brought him to Your disciples, but they could not cure him." Then Jesus answered and said, "O faithless and perverse generation, how long shall I be with you? How long shall I bear with you? Bring him here to Me." And Jesus rebuked the demon, and he came out of him; and the child was cured from that very hour. Then the disciples came to Jesus privately and said, "Why could we not cast him out?" So Jesus said to them, "Because of your unbelief; for assuredly, I say to you, if you have faith as a mustard seed, you will say to this mountain, 'Move from here to there,' and it will move; and nothing will be impossible for you. However, this kind does not go out except by prayer and fasting" (Matt. 17:14-21).*

What is the Gift of Faith? It could be the supernatural gift of casting out demons. In Mark 16, when Jesus listed the Sign Gifts, He listed *"casting out demons"*. I notice that it is not mentioned in the lists of gifts in Romans 12 and I Corinthians 12 or in I Peter 4. The other gifts are mentioned, why don't we see this gift there? If it is one of the miraculous Sign Gifts used to attest to the veracity of the apostle's message that we now have in written form (if that is the **only** meaning), I don't believe we have this gift with us anymore.

But is that all that is here? It also says, *"... all things are possible."* When things seem impossible, there are those among God's people who inspire confidence and say, "Yes, it can be done." There are some who have great faith and we see them among us today.

Also, it mentions prayer and fasting. When we find someone like this among God's people, we need to channel our prayer requests to them so we can get more answers. This

is a possibility. In Matthew 20, we see this gift again, and here it is not casting out a demon, and so we can conclude that this gift is not always connected with casting out a demon.

> *Now in the morning, as He returned to the city, He was hungry. And seeing a fig tree by the road, He came to it and found nothing on it but leaves, and said to it, "Let no fruit grow on you ever again." And immediately the fig tree withered away. Now when the disciples saw it, they marveled, saying, "How did the fig tree wither away so soon?" So Jesus answered and said to them, "Assuredly, I say to you, if you have faith and do not doubt, you will not only do what was done to the fig tree, but also if you say to this mountain, 'Be removed and be cast into the sea,' it will be done. And all things, whatever you ask in prayer, believing, you will receive" (Matt. 21:18-22).*

Here we have more support for our idea that the Gift of Faith is vitally connected with prayer — the ability to trust God, the ability to have a mountain moved out of the way. When we pray for things that seem impossible, we need faith to believe that God will answer our prayers. God has done these kinds of things and it is closely associated with prayer. The Gift of Faith is the ability to trust God in a difficult circumstance.

In the Faith Chapter (Hebrews 11), we see the life and death of many of God's special saints, and it ends this way, *"... these all died in faith."* These people had the ability to trust God in difficult circumstances — so difficult that their lives were taken from them.

It seems to me that the Gift of Faith is most often aptly described in the context of prayer. Even the healing described in James 5 is within the context of prayer.

> *The prayer of faith will save the sick (James 5:15).*

This is a special prayer ministry. It is possible to believe God for great things and to see Him do it, even though people don't think it is going to happen — *"... all things are possible."* This is very important.

There are those among God's people who are able to believe that God is going to do great things, and they go off to a private place and pray about it. That's what the Gift of Faith is.

The Gift of Discernment

This gift is the most misunderstood and misused gift in today's church. People say, "I know what you're thinking!" But even **I** don't know what I'm thinking most of the time. Only God knows what I'm thinking. The Bible says that we can't know what is in the hearts of others. We need to ask what the Gift of Discernment really is.

> *Let two or three prophets speak, and let the others judge (discern the spirits) (I Cor. 14:29).*

This gift was given at the time when God's prophets were speaking and it was given as a check on the Gift of Prophecy to discern whether a prophet was speaking from God or from the enemy.

It is also used for telling the difference between right and wrong. God gives some people to see what is right and wrong even when things are confusing.

> *For everyone who partakes only of milk is unskilled in the word of righteousness, for he is a babe. But solid food belongs to those who are of full age, that is, those who by reason of use have their senses exercised to discern both good and evil (Heb. 5:13-14).*

It literally means *"to divide"* and has the meaning of being able to make a distinction between things. When a prophet spoke, one with the Gift of Discernment could tell whether or not the prophecy was from God. Here the one with the Gift of Discernment can tell whether a thing is right or wrong when there is confusion about a matter.

> *I say this to your shame. Is it so, that there is not a wise man among you,*
> *not even one, who will be able to judge (discern) between his brethren?*
> *(Heb. 6:5).*

This is Christian arbitration and the Gift of Discerning shows up here again. It seems close to being a test of spirits. All of us are to test the spirits, but some among us have a gift to be able to understand the attitude behind what is said. Some think the gift is to know the different attitudes of people. I don't know exactly what it is. I don't know if it is discernment between God and Satan, or the ability to know attitudes, or the ability to know what is right in a legal situation. Clearly, though, it is the ability to see things that other people don't see. Discernment is very needed.

The Gift of Ministering,

The Gift of Showing Mercy,

The Gift of Faith

The Gift of Discernment

Gifts of Support

The Gift of Helps

This is not the same as the Gift of Ministry or Serving that we saw in Romans 12. A different word is used and I believe that a different gift is intended. The Gift of **Serving** is not people-oriented. It is rather task-oriented. Some people don't enjoy being involved with people, but they like to get a job done when they see a need.

There is another kind of person who is very sensitive and often gets hurt. The Gift of Helps **is** people-oriented rather than task-oriented. One meaning of the word is *"to take the place of someone"* and it must be motivated by helping someone else. The noun is used only once, and the verb is used three times, but in the Greek translation of the Old Testament it is used many times and it is very revealing.

It is often translated *"to bear the burden with someone"*. They often say, "How can I help you?" The service person sees a job and wants to get it done, but the *"helps"* person wants to bear the burden of someone else. They are motivated by relieving someone else. They want to be needed by someone who is overloaded. Nothing makes them happier than to take the load off someone and see them use their gifts in a more productive way. There are lots of people in the body of Christ just like this.

Moses was choosing leaders to help him in judging the people.

> *And let them judge the people at all times. Then it will be that every great matter they shall bring to you, but every small matter they themselves shall judge. So it will be easier for you, for they will **bear the burden with you** (Ex. 18:22).*

This is the Gift of Helps.

When this person sees someone who is overloaded, he offers to help carry the load. The motivation is very important. This person must help someone else. If a helper undermines the authority of the person they are helping and takes things over, then that person doesn't have the Gift of Helps because this gift always wants to help someone else - never to take things over.

This is a very helpful gift. It is literally helping someone else accomplish THEIR task. You don't have to have a task yourself in order to have a spiritual gift. You can be a helper-type of person.

> *Then I will come down and talk with you there. I will take of the Spirit that is upon you (Moses) and I will put the same upon them; and they shall bear the burden of the people with you, that you may not bear it yourself alone (Num. 11:17).*

"Bear the burden of the people" is the same word *"helps"* that we saw in the New Testament. This is important in the body of Christ. I don't believe in "Lone Rangers" in the body of Christ. It is a great fallacy to think that we can do something by ourselves and we don't need anyone to help. In that case, the growth of the Church would be limited by your abilities and God's work could not go beyond you and your abilities. One of the greatest revelations in God's work is to see that you need help.

People with the Gift of Helps can be helpful to that brother that is overloaded without threatening or undermining him. That's the difference between the one who tries to help without the gift and the person who has the gift. He says, "I will bear the burden with you and you won't have to bear it alone." That's a really sweet thing. God knows that we need people with this gift.

> *And those who have believing masters, let them not despise them because they are brethren, but rather serve them because those who are benefited ("helped") are believers and beloved (I Tim. 6:2).*

Christians who work for other Christians are not to resent them. They are not to kick back and take it easy because their boss (*"master"*) will "understand". No! They are *"to adorn the Gospel"* and try to make their boss' business profitable. I've heard Christians say that the boss makes enough, but these employees should be helping that business to be profitable.

Some of us seem to have the attitude that making money is carnal, but the carnality comes from WANTING to be rich whether we actually are or not. We can have money and not be carnal if we use it for the Lord and His causes. God can use those who have money for His purposes.

Also, God wants us to realize how He distributes His wealth to people. Some people have the ability to make money, and we should encourage them to make money but still not put their trust in *"uncertain riches"*. After all, missionaries need money. Our churches need money to operate. Money is a necessary tool in the work of the Lord. Don't try to keep good people from making money! They are the ones who will give to God's work and use that money to be a blessing to many.

If you have the Gift of Helps, you don't need to be in the limelight. You love to promote someone else who is doing God's work and you love to help them in their work.

> *"And now brethren" [says Paul], "I commend you to God and to the word of His grace, which is able to build you up and give you an inheritance among all those who are sanctified. I have coveted no one's silver or gold or apparel. Yes, you yourselves know that these hands have provided for my necessities, and for those who were with me. I have shown you in every way, by laboring like this, that you must support the weak. And remember the words of the Lord Jesus, that He said, 'It is more blessed to give than to receive.'"*

A lot of people say that this demonstrates that Paul had the Gift of Giving. Wait a minute! When he said, *"I've shown you"* ... by what I've done *"... that you must support the weak"* that word *"support"* is our word *"helps"* which we have seen in other Scriptures. It is more the Gift of Helps than the Gift of Giving. Paul had been willing to work and supply the needs of others (*"those who were with me"*) and he found joy in doing so. It is truly the Gift of Helps to enjoy helping someone else succeed. We can encourage people in the use of this gift.

The Gift of Giving

... he who gives, with liberality ...
(Rom. 12:8).

The word used for *"giving"* is interesting; it means *"to share with"* and paints a picture for us of what the gift really is.

Sometimes those who have the Gift of Giving have to be motivated by those in need. That is not always understood. Some people are "turned off" when I present a project that needs support, but find themselves interested when they hear of **a person** who has a need. How do you explain that? The motivation is a person in need.

God is a God of variety. We need to understand that the Spirit moves some people to give to one thing and others to give to something else. The project may be wonderful, but those who want to give to an individual's need will not be motivated by the project like they would be motivated by hearing a personal need of missionaries or pastors or of fellow believers. There are different kinds of *"givers"*. We are all different in the body of Christ.

The Gift of Giving is one that is motivated primarily by people rather than by projects or tasks. This gift responds to the needs of people.

> *Let him who stole steal no longer, but rather let him labor, working with his hands what is good, that he may have something to give him who has need (Eph. 4:28).*

There is another qualifying factor to know if you have the Gift of Giving or not. Romans 12 says, *"... with liberality"*. It means *"single"* in contrast to another word that means *"double"*. It might refer to singleness of mind and purpose; that is, you aren't giving to be seen of people — you're just giving because there is a need. The great joy of this kind of giver is that they are thrilled to be able to meet a need.

These people are sensitive, however. They resent the feeling that they have been manipulated into giving without the personal response of those whose needs have been met. Let's learn a lesson — the person with the Gift of Giving is moved by knowing what needs to be done; that person doesn't have to be manipulated into giving.

> *For I **long** to see you, that I may impart (share with) you some spiritual gift, so that you may be established (Rom. 1:11).*

So often we think of cash only when we think of the Gift of Giving. Another motivation for giving is a need that is met with what we have. Sometimes this means sharing our car or our home with people because we want to see people encouraged and a car or a place to stay are what they need at the moment.

> *So, affectionately longing for you, we were **well pleased** to impart (share with) you not only the gospel of God, but also our own lives, because you had become dear to us (I Thess. 2:8).*

All of the gifts can be used in evangelism even though we often think of them only within the body of Christ. Here is a verse, however, which clearly states that the Gift of

Giving is for sharing with the lost *"the gospel of God"*. This gift may be used to give to meet the needs of a neighbor during a tough time in their lives in order to get the opportunity to share the Gospel with them.

Paul says here that they were *"pleased"* to share the gospel and also their *"own lives"* because they had a loving relationship with them. This is another motivation of the Gift of Giving. *"... because you had become dear to us ...."* The very word *"share with"* indicates that there is **a people relationship** with those who are in need.

> *So let each one give as he purposes in his heart, not grudgingly or of necessity; for God loves a cheerful giver (II Cor. 9:7).*

"Cheerful" here means *"hilarious"* and the giver should find great joy in exercising this gift.

The Gift of Hospitality

A lot of people don't see this as a gift, but I believe the Scripture is clear in presenting it as a gift.

Be hospitable to one another without grumbling. As each one has received a gift, minister it to one another, as good stewards of the manifold grace of God (I Peter 4:9-10).

This verse (9) is connected to verse 10 by a conjunction and we must take note of that because the train of thought is connected. We are to *"minister to one another"* AS we are to *"be hospitable"* — that is, *"without grumbling"*. That's one of the reasons I believe there really is a Gift of Hospitality.

The word *"hospitality"* itself is a combination of words that means *"the love of strangers"*. It refers to someone who can meet strangers easily and make them feel comfortable. That is a spiritual gift. Hospitality is a real key to ministering to strangers. This gift makes people feel comfortable right away and they don't understand why they are right at home so quickly in a strange environment. That's the Gift of Hospitality.

> *Let love be without hypocrisy. ... distributing to the needs of the saints, given to hospitality (Rom. 12:9, 13).*

"Given to" here is a strong word meaning *"to pursue"* hospitality. These people don't take it lightly. They are actively looking for people who need to be ministered to with hospitality. They want to meet them and get acquainted with them. This is an exciting gift.

We're all to minister in all the gifts whether this is our special gift or not. We are all to be hospitable, too.

> *Do not forget to entertain strangers, for by so doing some have unwittingly entertained angels (Heb. 13:2).*

Abraham had this experience when three fellows came to visit him and he invited them to stay for a meal. One of them stayed behind and it turned out to be the Lord Himself. Abraham and Sarah didn't know they were angels. They were just strangers to whom they offered a meal.

Wouldn't it be great to be in a church where people just like to invite people over to their home? And I Peter makes it clear that we are to do this *"without grumbling"* or complaining. We can't count who has had us to their home in return or not. We can't complain if something gets spilled or broken. The Gift of Hospitality can be dangerous, especially if your guests have children!

Sign Gifts

One of the purposes of God's giving spiritual gifts is to give evidence or proof that the ministry and message of the apostles was truly by God and from God.

> *Therefore we must give the more earnest heed to the things we have heard, lest we drift away. For if the word spoken through angels proved steadfast, and every transgression and disobedience received a just reward, how shall we escape if we neglect so great a salvation, which at the first began to be spoken by the Lord, and was confirmed to us by those who heard Him, God also bearing witness both with signs and wonders, with various miracles, and gifts of the Holy Spirit, according to His own will? (Heb. 2:1-4).*

Now according to this text, the gifts of the Holy Spirit were bearing witness to the message of the apostles who heard Christ. In Hebrews 2:4, the gifts are called *"signs"*, *"wonders"*, and *"miracles"*.

There's a great misunderstanding among God's people today over the whole issue of the miraculous sign gifts, and what they were for.

Jesus had just given the great commission to His disciples on the very night that He arose from the dead. Now it says,

> *And these signs will follow (or accompany) those who believe: In my name they will cast out demons; they will speak with new tongues; they will take up serpents; and if they drink anything deadly, it will by no means hurt them; they will lay hands on the sick and they will recover (Mk. 16:17-18).*

Here we're talking about signs — miraculous signs. Now, look at the next two verses.

> *So then, after the Lord had spoken to them, He was received up into heaven, and sat down at the right hand of God. And they went out and preached everywhere, the Lord working with them, and confirming the word through the accompanying signs (Mk. 16:19-20).*

The Bible is very clear. The miraculous signs that are listed in Mark 16 were intended to confirm that the message they spoke was truly from God. It *"confirm[ed] the word through the accompanying signs."*

The word *"signs"* appears 77 times in the New Testament, and the truth of the matter is that the Bible evidence shows that (in addition to the apostles) there were only two men who ever did any of these signs, Stephen and Philip. There is no record that anyone else ever did any of these signs.

If you believe that you have the spiritual gift of healing (the Lord said, *"They will lay hands on the sick, and they will recover"*), that when you touch the sick, they're healed, then you should go down to the local hospital and clean it out. I'm serious! I'm not being facetious. If you have that gift, and you have any sort of compassion and mercy at all, I don't understand why you don't go where the sick people are and heal them.

I absolutely believe God can heal people, and I've seen it happen. Have I ever seen anybody with that power in his hand today? Absolutely not. No one even comes close. A lot of people proclaim themselves to be healers. They'll even have meetings in which you can watch them heal people on television. The Bible says that anyone who was touched by Jesus was absolutely healed.

Many of the self-proclaimed healers say that people have to have faith, so if they aren't healed, they tell them they didn't have enough faith. That gets the healer off the hook. The problem is that the Bible doesn't teach that either. Jesus healed people that didn't even believe in Him. It isn't necessary for the sick person to have faith in order to have a healing take place. If the healing comes from God, He is not limited by whether or not you believe. He can do whatever He wants to do.

Let's see what the Bible says about these miraculous signs. We see Peter preaching on the Day of Pentecost.

> *"Men of Israel, hear these words: Jesus of Nazareth, a Man attested by God to you by miracles, wonders and signs which God did through Him in your midst, as you yourselves also know - Him, being delivered by the determined counsel and foreknowledge of God, you have taken by lawless hands, have crucified, and put to death; whom God raised up, having loosed the pains of death, because it was not possible that He should be held by it (Acts 2:22-24).*

Isn't that interesting? In Hebrews 2, the apostles who heard Christ were affirmed and attested to by miraculous wonders and signs. According to the Bible, so was Jesus. The credentials of Jesus that He was the Messiah were the *"miracles, wonders and signs"* which He did. These signs proved that He was who He claimed — that He was truly the Messiah.

> *Then fear came upon every soul, and many wonders and signs were done through the apostles (Acts 2:43).*

And through the hands of the apostles many signs and wonders were done among the people. And they were all with one accord in Solomon's Porch (Acts. 5:12).

"He (God) brought them out, after He had shown wonders and signs in the land of Egypt, and in the Red Sea, and in the wilderness forty years (Acts. 7:36).

We're talking about miracles here. God gave gifts to His people that were absolutely miraculous in nature and could not be explained in natural terms. Jesus mentioned what they were: Casting out demons, drinking deadly poison that won't hurt you, laying hands on the sick resulting in instantaneous recovery, and speaking in new languages. These miraculous signs were confirmation and proof of Jesus (that He's the Messiah), then of the apostles' message directly revealed to them by Jesus (that it was truly from God and should be added to the Old Testament revelation).

And Stephen, full of faith and power, did great wonders and signs among the people (Acts 6:8).

And the multitudes with one accord heeded the things spoken by Philip, hearing and seeing the miracles which he did (Acts. 8:6).

Then Simon himself also believed; and when he was baptized he continued with Philip, and was amazed, seeing the miracles and signs which were done (Acts. 8:13).

Therefore they stayed there a long time, speaking boldly in the Lord, who was bearing witness to the word of His grace, granting signs and wonders to be done by their hands (Acts. 14:3).

Then all the multitude kept silent and listened to Barnabas and Paul declaring how many miracles and wonders God had worked through them among the Gentiles (Acts. 15:12).

At the Council of Jerusalem, the Jews were saying, "Do you mean that Gentiles are in this church, too?" They got Paul and Barnabas down there to have a debate over whether the Gentiles should be let in or not. In the early days, the Jews were wondering about the Gentiles. God had given Paul a direct revelation that Jews and Gentiles should be one body in Christ. The early Jewish leaders never thought that was true. They thought it was going to be a Jewish church all the way, but *"the multitude kept silent"* and

heard about the *"many miracles and wonders God had worked through them among the Gentiles."*

That was the proof, that was the evidence that they were truly apostles of our Lord and Savior, Jesus Christ.

Paul said his ministry of apostleship was known by *"mighty signs, wonders and miracles"* (Rom. 15:19).

I have heard all the arguments in the Christian world today about how individual believers can do these miraculous deeds, but I have yet to see the evidence in the Scripture. The purpose for the miraculous signs and wonders in the life of Christ was to prove He was the Messiah. In the apostles who heard Him, it was to prove that their message was truly given to them by the Lord.

Signs and Wonders

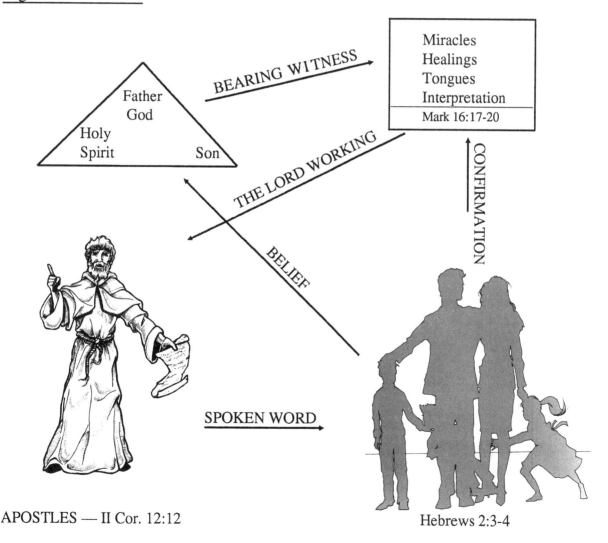

APOSTLES — II Cor. 12:12   Hebrews 2:3-4

The Gift of Miracles

The issue at stake is not whether or not miracles take place. Healings and miracles take place today. The issue is a question of method, not of fact. How does God perform miracles and healings today?

Is it through specific individuals who have been gifted ...

... or do healings and miracles today occur apart from gifted individuals?

Miracles Are A Sign Gift

The Gift of Miracles, the very word *"miracles"*, is used 120 times in the New Testament. The root word stresses the ability to do something supernatural, contrary to natural law or explanation. This word is translated *"power, mighty deed, might, strength"* and with several other words. There are about six forms of the word used in connection with miracles, power and strength. The emphasis, however, is always on the source of power, not on the display of power.

The word *"miracle"* refers to the following:

Miracles of Jesus in Luke 4:36 and in Acts 2:22,

God's power to save in Romans 1:16,

Human strength and ability in Matthew 25:15,

Power in Jesus in Mark 5:30,

Power of the Holy Spirit to believers in Acts 1:8,

Miracles of the Apostles in Acts 3:12, Hebrews 2:4, and II Corinthians 12:12,

Strength of sin in I Corinthians 15:56, and

Power of angels and demons in II Thessalonians 1:7.

The Gift of Miracles is defined as the ability to perform supernatural acts which clearly demonstrate God's power as being greater than that of Satan.

The Gift of Miracles is one of the sign gifts. According to Hebrews 2:4, it is one of the *"signs, wonders and miracles"* that God used to confirm His word, and some of those miracles are enumerated in Mark, chapter 16. It is also clearly stated by Paul:

Truly the signs of an apostle were accomplished among you with all perseverance, in signs and wonders and mighty deeds (miracles) (II Cor. 12:12).

It was one of the sign gifts, not only in the lives of the apostles, and also in the life of Jesus Christ:

"Men of Israel, hear these words: Jesus of Nazareth, a Man attested by God to you by miracles, wonders, and signs which God did through Him in your midst, as you yourselves also know" (Acts 2:22).

The Bible says that miracles gave attestation, proof, and confirmation that Jesus was really who He claimed to be. According to the prophet Isaiah, Jesus (as Messiah) would **have to** heal the blind, the lame, the dumb and the deaf. He would also have to raise the dead. According to John 20:30-31, the signs and miracles that Jesus did were given to us to prove that Jesus is the Messiah, the Son of God.

Jesus did many miracles and signs. John 21:25 says that it would not even be possible for all the world's books to contain what He did. He did many, many miracles, but notice that they were done in order to prove who He is. He's the Messiah, and He was fulfilling prophecy by doing miracles.

In the Scripture, two things are specifically called *"miracles"*. That doesn't mean that other acts of Jesus are not miracles. They were certainly miraculous. For instance, walking on the water was miraculous. Feeding the 5,000 was miraculous, but when you study the word *"miracle"*, you discover that only two things are called miracles: One is the casting out of unclean spirits. Casting demons out of people is called a *"miracle"*.

Casting Out Demons

So they were all amazed and spoke among themselves, saying, "What a word this is! For with authority and power (that's our word "miracle") He commands the unclean spirits, and they come out" (Luke 4:36).

But Jesus said, "Do not forbid him (a person who is casting out demons in His name), for no one who works a miracle in My name can soon afterward speak evil of Me" (Mark 9:39).

It's clear in this text that *"casting out a demon"* IS the *"working of a miracle"*. It was one of the things that a worker of miracles did. He cast demons out. Jesus, of course, did that.

The Miracle of Healing

The second thing that the word *"miracle"* applies to is the matter of healing. That's why we have the gift of miracles and healings together. They are two separate gifts, and the word *"miracle"* can't be restricted to *"healing"*, but the word *"miracle"* does include *"healing"*.

Now He could do no mighty work ("miracle") there (in Nazareth), except that He laid His hands on a few sick people and healed them (Mark 6:5).

Obviously, laying hands on sick people and healing them is the working of a *"miracle"* as this text clearly indicates. It was not only one of the sign gifts, but miracles were done by several people in the New Testament besides Jesus.

Who Worked Miracles?

I want to look at the Scripture for my answers, don't you? I want to know what the Bible says. A lot of people today seem to intimate that many of the average believers of the New Testament were working miracles, so let's look into the Bible and ask, "Who worked miracles?"

In addition to Jesus, we know that the twelve disciples worked miracles.

> *Then He called His twelve disciples together and gave them power and authority over all demons, and to cure diseases (Luke 9:1).*

It is interesting that those two things often go together. He gave them *"authority over demons"*, and secondly, *"to cure diseases"*. So the twelve apostles were healing people. It's interesting that the twelve disciples at this point include Judas. Do you believe that Judas cast out demons and healed people? According to the Bible he did. It says, "the twelve disciples." We know from the Scriptures that Judas was never a believer, yet he had the ability to cast out a demon and to heal people.

You can add another group who did miracles. There was a special group called *"the seventy"*.

> *After these things the Lord appointed seventy others also, and sent them two by two before His face into every city and place where He Himself was about to go. Then He said to them, "... And heal the sick who are there." Then the seventy returned with joy, saying, "Lord, even the demons are subject to us in Your name" (Luke 10:1, 9, 17).*

Evidently they cast out demons and healed people, exactly like the twelve apostles.

The *"seventy"* are mentioned three times in the Old Testament. Genesis 46:27 says that *"seventy souls"* came to Egypt, but in the Greek translation of that passage it says seventy-two. A second time it is mentioned is Exodus 1:5 where it tells about the exodus, it mentions *"seventy"* again. Again, in the Greek Old Testament, it says seventy-two. In Deuteronomy 10:22 we have a prooftext as to whether or not there were seventy or seventy-two.

*"Your fathers went down to Egypt with seventy persons, and now the Lord
your God has made you as the stars of heaven in multitude" (Deut. 10:22).*

Interesting that the Greek translation of the Old Testament is not consistent. In the
Genesis and Exodus passages they mention seventy-two, but here it is seventy. So it con-
tradicts itself. The Hebrew text clearly has seventy in all three cases.

Now in the book of Acts in chapter six when Stephen gives his address, he indicates
that there were seventy-five, not seventy. The whole issue deals with counting children. If
you read the text carefully, there are sixty-six, not seventy or seventy-five. There are
sixty-six who came out of the loins of Jacob. Now the Bible is very clear in Genesis, you
add Jacob and you add Joseph and his two sons, and that brings you to seventy. How do
you get to seventy-five? Joseph had other children. They are added in Stephen's address,
but they are not mentioned in the original seventy in the Old Testament.

Why seventy? The Jews teach that there are seventy heads of Jewish families, that
came out of Abraham, Isaac and Jacob. At the time of our Lord, Josephus the Jewish his-
torian mentions that there were seventy, not seventy-two. Why do we care?

Jesus did miracles to prove that He is Messiah. The twelve disciples did miracles
under the authority of Christ to continue to demonstrate His Messiahship, and the seventy
had a special purpose by God, to do the exact same thing while penetrating all of the
family heads of Israel. Jesus chose seventy because he wanted every family, every clan to
hear the message that the kingdom of heaven is at hand. In order to prove that this message is the message of the Messiah, they had to do miracles, cast out demons, and heal
people.

*And when He had called His twelve disciples to Him, He gave them power
over unclean spirits, to cast them out, and to heal all kinds of sickness and
all kinds of diseases. These twelve Jesus sent out and commanded them,
saying: "Do not go into the way of the Gentiles, and do not enter a city of
the Samaritans. But go rather to the lost sheep of the house of Israel"
(Matt. 10:1, 5).*

It's clear when Jesus appointed the twelve to cast out demons and heal people, they
had a special ministry only to the house of Israel. When He sent out the seventy, they
were to do exactly the same thing, cast out demons, heal people, and it was a special message to the House of Israel, the seventy heads of the families. They had the accrediting
signs to prove that Jesus really was the Messiah. That was their only mission and that's
why there's no mention of them again in the Scriptures.

It was very important because the Jews require a sign. The Jews knew from the Old
Testament that they were to see the miracles in order to believe that Jesus truly was the

Messiah. Isaiah long ago had predicted that He would do these miracles. So we have Jesus, the twelve, the seventy who did miracles.

In Hebrew 2:4 the word miracles is put with signs and wonders. The same thing is found in II Cor. 12:12 — *"signs, wonders and miracles"*. They go together. In Acts 6:8, though, it does not say that Stephen did any miracles. However, I think it is obvious that he did by the usage of the two words that usually accompany miracles.

> *And Stephen, full of faith and power, did great wonders and signs among the people (Acts 6:8).*

What are the sign gifts? They are miracles, healings, tongues, and interpretation of tongues. The Bible says Stephen did *"great wonders"* and *"signs"*. Those are also called miracles. So I have to add Stephen into this camp.

Another person who did miracles was Philip. Stephen and Philip were two of the seven chosen by the early church in Jerusalem to care for the widows who were being neglected in the distribution of food.

> *And the multitude with one accord heeded the things spoken by Philip, hearing and seeing the miracles which he did. For unclean spirits, crying with a loud voice, came out of many who were possessed; and many who were paralyzed and lame were healed (Acts 8:6-7).*

Again, we see casting out demons and healing people. So Philip is added to our list, and we also add Paul.

> *Now God worked unusual miracles by the hands of Paul, so that even handkerchiefs or aprons were brought from his body to the sick, and the diseases left them and the evil spirits went out of them (Acts. 19:11-12).*

Notice again that miracles is described as sickness and evil spirits going out. The Bible says that even handkerchiefs were brought from his (Paul's) body to the sick. The Bible is very clear that Paul even in his day was doing something extraordinary, very unusual. The average person working miracles wasn't doing this. This is the only mention of this anywhere. An unusual thing happened and God blessed it and God was again attesting the fact that these apostles were truly from God. We should not be deceived by those who say they are doing this today.

The Gift of Healing

Does God heal today? Absolutely!

Does God heal through people with the Gift of Healing?   That's highly questionable.

Let's take a look at it from the Scripture and see for ourselves. First of all, the word for *"healing"* as compared to the Gift of Healing. The Greek word is used 34 times and is very different from the common word for healing which is like our English word *"therapeutic"*. *"Therapeutic"* really deals with the care of an individual as the healing is taking place. The emphasis is on the care of the needs of the sick. It is not as strong a term as the first term, which is referring to the miracle itself.

Another interesting thing: when you apply *"therapeutic"* healing, it is not always clear that it's an instantaneous, miraculous healing. It can apply to the process and gradual therapy involved in the healing — the care of the sick that brings the healing. The other Greek word, which is used 34 times, is used for an instantaneous act—healing occurs instantaneously, and full restoration occurs. That's interesting, because when the Bible gives us the name of the gift, it uses the word which means the instantaneous, absolute restoration of that individual, right on the spot!

Let me give you some things about the healings:

Number one - it's one of the sign gifts (Mark 16:18 - *"they will lay hands on the sick, and they will recover."*)

Number two - healings were done by Jesus, the twelve, the seventy, Philip, Peter, and Paul. Let's just mention Peter for a moment. First in Acts 3, Peter healed a lame man. In Acts 5:15-16 it says,

> So they brought the sick out into the streets and laid them on beds and couches, that at least the shadow of Peter passing by might fall on some of them. Also a multitude gathered from the surrounding cities to Jerusalem, bringing sick people and those who were tormented by unclean spirits, and they also were all healed.

I have all kinds of people telling me today that it isn't necessary for someone with the gift of healing to heal everyone who comes to him for healing. I have a problem with that. Jesus had the Gift of Healing. The Bible says over and over again that **all who came to Him** were healed by Him. That's quite a statement. There were a lot of people sick who obviously didn't make it, but all who were brought to Him were healed.

Matt. 8:16 says that He healed **all who were sick.**

Luke 16:19 says He healed them **all.**

Matthew 15 says the exact same thing.

Jesus Christ healed all who came to Him.

Now when I look at Peter, it says that they were **all healed,** and he has so much power he doesn't even have to touch them but just walk by so his shadow touches them. This is miraculous! And then Paul healed people with the handkerchiefs taken from his body to the sick. Let's face it, these are unusual things that are happening.

Peter healed the lame man, he healed many demon posessed sick people in this chapter. Look at chapter 9, verse 33. He healed a paralyzed man just like Jesus did. The man had been bed-ridden for eight years, and he was paralyzed — probably with a stroke. Verse 34 says,

> And Peter said to him, "Aeneas, Jesus the Christ heals you. Arise and make your bed." Then he arose immediately. So all who dwelt at Lydda and Sharon saw him and turned to the Lord (Acts. 9:34).

Now in this same text he also raised a woman from the dead. Verse 37 says,

> But it happened in those days that she became sick and died. But Peter put them all out, and knelt down and prayed. And turning to the body he said, "Tabitha, arise." And she opened her eyes, and when she saw Peter she sat up. Then he gave her his hand and lifted her up; and when he had called the saints and widows, he presented her alive. And it became known throughout all Joppa, and many believed on the Lord (Acts 9:37, 40).

Let's face it, Peter did some amazing miracles.

Miraculous things happened to these people. But now when I hear about healing today, all of a sudden we only heal people on certain occasions (?!?!?). First, we heal them when we called a meeting for it. Now, seriously, if you believe that someone today has the gift that was in the New Testament, wouldn't it be natural to assume that all those who we brought to them would be healed? If they had that gift and they had any sort of compassion, wouldn't you think they would go to the hospitals and clean them out?

They say the reason certain people don't get healed is that the sick person doesn't have enough faith! Once again, we're denying what the Bible says. Jesus healed people who didn't have any faith. They were unbelievers. Do you believe it is necessary for you to have faith in order to get healed? That is not necessary at all. God can heal any time He wants to. God is not limited by my faith. He called people of "little faith" and miraculous things happened, and some of us have very little faith, but God does not depend on our faith to do a miraculous deed. He just does it. He can do anything He wants to do, any time He wants to do it.

I believe God heals, but not necessarily in the format we so often see, which is organized, theatrical, and highly emotional, with the "healer" commanding that God heal the person. Nowhere in the Bible is God **commanded** to heal. So many dear people go through that and are not healed, and then they go around feeling guilty because they were told they didn't have enough faith. It is an insult to God.

The Gift of Tongues

Identification of the Gift

1. Grammatical Meaning - *"gene glosson"*

I'd like you to notice the name of this gift. It's called, *"kindS of tongueS"* — both words are plural. When people say, "I have the gift of a tongue", I believe they are mistaken in the name of the spiritual gift. The name of the gift is *"kindS of tongueS"*. We get our word *"generation"* from this Greek word. It refers to *"families of tongues"* — groupings of tongues or languages.

> *And God has appointed these in the church: first, apostles, second prophets, third teachers, after that miracles, then gifts of healings, helps, administrations, varieties of tongues. Are all apostles? Are all prophets? Are all teachers? Are all workers of miracles? Do all have gifts of healings? Do all speak with tongues? Do all interpret? (I Cor. 12:28-30).*

Each of these questions assumes a negative answer.

There are three basic usages of the word *"tongue"*:

> a. the organ of taste,
>
> b. speech or language,
>
> c. a manner of speaking which needs explanation.

2. Biblical Usage

The word appears 50 times in the New Testament. The word *"dialektos"* is translated *"tongue"* in Acts 1:19, 2:8, 21:40, 22;2 and 26:14.

The references to the spiritual gift of tongues are found in:

> Mark 16:17
>
> I Cor. 12:10, 28, 30; Acts 2:3, 4, 11
>
> I Cor. 13:1, 8; Acts 10:46
>
> I Cor. 14:2, 4-6, 9, 13-14, 18-19,
>
> Acts 19:6, 22-23, 26-27, 39

3. Definition - The ability to speak in foreign languages without any previous knowledge of that language.

Usage of the Gift

In Mark 16:17, Jesus tells us that people will speak in *"new"* tongues. In Greek there are two words for *"new"* - one *"new"* from the standpoint of time, the other *"new"* in the sense of being new to the experience of the person. In Mark 16:17 Jesus is saying the languages will be new to the experience of the person — not languages that are new from the standpoint of time.

1. Day of Pentecost

> *Now when the Day of Pentecost had fully come, they were all with one accord in one place. And suddenly there came a sound from heaven, as of a rushing mighty wind, and it filled the whole house where they were sitting. Then there appeared to them divided tongues, as of fire, and one sat upon each of them. And they were all filled with the Holy Spirit and began to speak with other tongues, as the Spirit gave them utterance (Acts 2:1-4).*

It doesn't say that it WAS *"a rushing mighty wind"*. It says it was LIKE *"a rushing mighty wind"*. It says there was an APPEARANCE of tongues — it doesn't say there WERE tongues of fire sitting on them. There were about a hundred and twenty people there (Acts 1:15). Pictures showing only the twelve with tongues of fire on their heads is not quite accurate. It appears that ALL of them were involved (see vs.4).

There are two words in Greek for *"another"* - one is *"another of the same kind"* and the other is *"another of a different kind"*. This word used when they *"began to speak with other tongues"* is *"another of a different kind"* — it was different from their normal speech or language. These were not language structures that were familiar to them; they were completely different. The Word of God is very clear on that point.

> *And when this sound occurred, the multitude came together, and were confused, because everyone heard them speak in his own language (Acts 2:6).*

"Language" here is the word for dialect and everybody understands what that means. Everyone heard in his own language. Some even argue that this is a miracle of hearing rather than a miracle of speaking. The only point I see in such an argument would be to get away from the problem of speaking in a foreign language. It is clear, however, that the people heard in their own unique dialects and languages.

"And how is it that we hear, each in our own language (dialect) in which we were born?" (Acts 2:8).

"We hear them speaking in our own tongues the wonderful works of God" (Acts. 2:11).

It seems to me that no one can argue that the tongues of Acts 2 were anything but foreign languages. If we're going to be faithful to God's Word, the Holy Spirit has clarified (at least in Acts 2) that tongues were speaking in foreign languages which was not similar to the language of the speaker — it was another of a different kind.

2. Samaritan believers - Simon "saw" something when they received the Holy Spirit.

Now when the apostles who were at Jerusalem heard that Samaria had received the word of God, they sent Peter and John to them, who, when they had come down, prayed for them that they might receive the Holy Spirit. For as yet He had fallen upon none of them. They had only been baptized in the name of the Lord Jesus. Then they laid hands on them, and they received the Holy Spirit. Now when Simon saw that through the laying on of the apostles' hands the Holy Spirit was given, he offered them money (Acts. 8:14-18).

3. House of Cornelius

For they heard them speak with tongues and magnify God (Acts 10:46).

In Acts 10:46, the Gentile believers spoke in tongues. Now, whatever happened there, I want you to notice this verse in which Peter is recounting what happened in Acts 10:

"And as I began to speak, the Holy Spirit fell upon them, AS UPON US AT THE BEGINNING. ... If therefore God gave them THE SAME GIFT AS HE GAVE US when we believed on the Lord Jesus Christ ...." (Acts 11:15, 17).

It seems to me that what happened in Acts 10 is the same as what happened in Acts 2. Therefore, I conclude that they also spoke in foreign languages in Acts 10 as they did in Acts 2. That seems obvious from Peter's account in Acts 11.

4. Twelve disciples at Ephesus - The fourth mention of tongues is found in Acts 19.

And it happened, while Apollos was at Corinth, that Paul, having passed through the upper regions, came to Ephesus. And finding some disciples he said to them, "Did you receive the Holy Spirit when you believed?" And they said to him, "We have not so much as heard as heard whether there is a Holy Spirit." And he said to them, "Into what then were you baptized?" So they said, "Into John's baptism." Then Paul said, "John indeed baptized with a baptism of repentance, saying to the people that they should believe on Him who would come after him, that is, on Christ Jesus." When they heard this, they were baptized in the name of the Lord Jesus. And when Paul had laid hands on them, the Holy Spirit came upon them, and they spoke with tongues and prophesied (Acts 19:1-6).

In the old King James, the language here makes it appear that the receiving of the Holy Spirit was subsequent — after the experience of believing. The Greek allows only the meaning, "Did you receive the Holy Spirit WHEN (at the moment) you believed?" It was not subsequent to their believing.

Remember that these people were disciples of John the Baptist. We know that because Apollos was a disciple of John the Baptist and they were the disciples of Apollos (Acts 18:25). John the Baptist was a forerunner of Jesus and these disciples had probably not heard of the death and resurrection of Jesus Christ. Apollos was an Alexandrian Jew and he went from Alexandria to Ephesus, so it is possible that he had not heard of the events of the death and resurrection of Christ. They did not know the New Testament teaching concerning the Holy Spirit.

And he (Paul) said to them, "Into what then were you baptized?" So they said, "Into John's baptism" (Acts. 19:3).

Now why would Christian baptism indicate a knowledge of the Holy Spirit's ministry? Two possible answers are:

1. The baptismal formula says, *"I baptize you in the name of the Father, and of the Son, and of the Holy Spirit."*

2. It may be referring to the baptism of the Holy Spirit by which we become members of the body of Christ.

John's baptism was all they knew.

Then Paul said, "John indeed baptized with a baptism of repentance, saying to the people they should believe on Him who would come after him, that is, on Christ Jesus." When they heard this, they were baptized in the name of the Lord Jesus. And when Paul had laid hands on them, the

Holy Spirit came upon them, and they spoke with tongues and prophesied.
Now the men were about twelve in all (Acts 19:4-6).

As we look at these people, we see that they were Jewish; they were disciples of John the Baptist; they did not know about the death and resurrection of Jesus Christ. Therefore, their speaking in tongues is very much like the speaking in tongues in Acts 2 and Acts 10. It is confirming the fact that they had received the Holy Spirit.

Non-Charismatics like to say that tongues are NOT the evidence of salvation. I'm not so sure about that. In Acts, tongues WERE a sign that people had received the Holy Spirit.

<u>5. Church at Corinth</u> - I Cor. 12-14

The only other references to the gift of tongues are found in I Corinthians 12, 13 and 14. In chapter twelve we have a list of nine of the gifts.

... to another the working of miracles, to another prophecy, to another discerning of spirits, to another different kinds of tongues, to another the interpretation of tongues (I Cor. 12:10).

Again, we have the usage of *"another"* with the word for *"another of the same kind"* in verse 8. However, when we come to *"faith"* in verse 9, it is *"another of a different kind"*, so there is something different about faith as it relates to wisdom and knowledge. When it says *"... to another gifts of healings"*, it says *"another of the same kind"*. Something about healing is like faith.

In verse 10, *"... to another the working of miracles"* is *"another of the same kind"* — like faith and healing. Prophecy is the same as miracles, faith and healing. Also, *"discerning of spirits"* is the same. But, when you come to the last two, the word changes to *"another of a different kind"* — *"... to another (of a different kind) tongues, and another (of the same kind) the interpretation of tongues."* Interpretation is like tongues.

There are three groupings separated by *"a different kind"* — the first has two in it (verse 8), the second has five in it (verses 9 and 10), and the last has two (tongues and interpretation of tongues). I do not know exactly what all this means. It's possible that they are interchangeable, but it's also possible that they are different in HOW they are used. I really don't know. I DO know, however, that when the Holy Spirit chooses words, He definitely separated the last two from the ones that went before.

Now, we must try to be careful with the Bible. All Christians should agree that (at least as it relates to the spiritual gifts) not ALL believers have this gift. Any teacher that insists that every believer speak in tongues is violating God's Word. There is no other way to view it. If the gift is here today and IF it is to be used by certain individuals, no

one has the grounds from the Bible to insist that every believer is to speak in tongues. That simply is not so.

In the love chapter (I Cor. 13), it says that *"love never fails"* (verse 8), but *"prophecies will fail and tongues will cease, knowledge will vanish away."* About prophecies and knowledge the word *"fail"* is used (*"vanish away"* is the same word). This word indicates that these are phased out over a period of time — they are not to end abruptly, but gradually over a period of time, they will come to an end. But of the gift of tongues, it says they will ***"cease"*** — that means that they will come to an abrupt stop. The tense of the Greek means that *"in and of themselves, they will cease"*.

People who care about this verse and its meaning say that those who claim that tongues are languages have a problem since languages have not ceased. However, I would point out that if it refers to the spiritual gift of speaking in languages you have not learned then that will stop, not languages as such. **When** the gift stopped is what we argue about!

USAGE OF TONGUES		
SCRIPTURE	PEOPLE	PLACE
ACTS 2:4-13	JEWS	JERUSALEM
ACTS 8:5-9, 17-19	SAMARITANS	SAMARIA
ACTS 10:44-48	GENTILES	CAESAREA
ACTS 19:1-7	DISCIPLES OF JOHN THE BAPTIST	EPHESUS
I COR. 12-14	LOCAL CHURCH	CORINTH

WHAT ARE TONGUES ?

Possible Viewpoints:

The ability to speak in foreign langueages
without previous knowledge of the language.

The ability to speak in ecstatic utterances
unrelated to the known languages of the world.

Foreign languages.

What is the Gift of Tongues?

The first of the three major viewpoints of gifts today is that the gift of tongues is the ability to speak in foreign languages without any previous knowledge of that language. It doesn't make any difference if you are charismatic in doctrine or not. There are Charismatics who believe that and there are non-Charismatics who believe that. Some like to call it "the missionary gift". It certainly would be vital to the spread of the gospel. If people have the ability to speak in another language they should come forth and use their gift to further the cause of Christ. That seems to me to be very important.

There are those who say this is the Gift of Tongues and that there is evidence of it today. I've seen books where case histories were given. These stories are quite difficult to document. One writer wrote a book concerning tongues speakers. The conclusion is very academic and this study was unable to establish any known language pattern among present day tongues speech. Charismatics said that proved that "the gift of tongues" was ecstatic utterances, not languages. Non-Charismatics used the SAME study to prove that the New Testament gift of tongues was languages !

The second viewpoint is probably the major viewpoint among Charismatic churches today. It is that "the Gift of Tongues" is an ecstatic utterance (a prayer language) which is unrelated to any known language of today. It is very difficult to deal with that viewpoint, or to attack it — or even to understand it. All the evidence that has been put down on paper offers no common elements. It seems to depend on who taught a person to speak in tongues to find common elements. Those who have listened to someone speak in tongues seem to follow the patterns they have heard, but it is almost impossible to find a common element in ALL ecstatic utterances.

The third major viewpoint is that foreign languages are in the Book of Acts and are the evidence of the baptism of the Holy Spirit, but ecstatic utterances are in I Corinthians. There is currently a strong movement to say that all believers need one experience of the Acts kind of gift, but only some believers have the kind of gift that continues on.

Within the main viewpoint, there are three variations:

1. Acts is evidence of the baptism of the Holy Spirit and I Corinthians is the spiritual gift that only some have. We just discussed this.

2. The foreign languages of Acts only indicate the coming of the Holy Spirit, but in I Corinthians there is a gift of ecstatic utterance for private edification which is being regulated (I Cor. 14) in terms of its public use. Churches today are splitting over this question. This chapter says that you can never have more than two or three speaking in tongues in the same service.

3. Foreign languages are in Acts and in I Corinthians. Ecstatic utterances represent what the carnal Corinthians were doing — counterfeiting the true spiritual gift. This is a prevalent view among non-Charismatics.

The true Gift of Tongues (in my view) is **always** foreign languages, and here are my reasons for believing this:

> a. That's the normal use for the word *"tongues"*.

> b. The references to *"dialect"* and *"birth"* in Acts 2:6 and 8 seem to me to be tremendous evidence that the true gift of tongues is speaking in foreign languages.

> c. The word *"kinds"* of tongues suggest families of languages. If it were ecstatic utterances, it would be hard to understand what this means, but if it is languages, the meaning is clear.

4. The fact that a gift of interpretation is needed suggests to me that it is foreign languages. Today, the gift of interpretation is used to paraphrase what was said, it is not a direct translation. That doesn't seem to bother Charismatic leaders. In John 1, we find the word *"interpretation"* used in the Bible.

> *Then Jesus turned, and seeing them following, said to them, "What do you seek?" They said to Him, "Rabbi" (which is to say, when translated, Teacher), "where are You staying?" (John 1:38).*

The word *"translated"* is the same as the exact word *"interpretation"* of tongues. Was it a direct translation? When you translate the word *"rabbi"*, it is *"teacher"*. There is no paraphrase here. This is a direct translation.

> *And he brought him to Jesus. Now when Jesus looked at him, He said, "You are Simon the son of Jonah. You shall be called Cephas" (which is translated, A Stone) (John 1:42).*

Is this a direct translation, or a paraphrase? It is clearly a direct translation.

> *And He said to him, "Go, wash in the pool of Siloam" (which is translated, Sent). So he went and washed, and came back seeing (John 9:7).*

Once again, it is a direct translation, not a paraphrase.

> *... to whom also Abraham gave a tenth part of all, first being translated "king of righteousness," and then also king of Salem, meaning "king of peace" (Heb. 7:2).*

The word *"Melchizedek"* has two words in it, *"king"* and *"righteousness"*. That is **directly translated** in this text. To those who say the interpretation can not only give just the meaning of an utterance, but also expand on it, I must tell you that I don't believe that. I'm not just saying that to be critical of those who believe it, but I think it's time someone told the truth.

If the gift of interpretation is here today, it should be a direct translation of someone speaking in a foreign language without previous knowledge of that language, not a paraphrase. This is very serious. It was so serious that Paul rebuked the Corinthian church for not giving a direct translation. He also told them they had no right to speak unless they had an interpreter.

5. The Old Testament is used as an illustration of tongues.

In the law it is written:

"With men of other tongues and other lips I will speak to this people; And yet, for all that, they will not hear Me," says the Lord. Therefore tongues are for a sign, not to those who believe but to unbelievers; but prophesying is not for unbelievers but for those who believe (I Cor. 14:21-22).

"Unbelievers" here are the Children of Israel who are not responding to God's prophets so God brought a nation to judge them. Jeremiah prophesied the same thing at another time in history. That clearly points out that tongues are foreign languages in both of these cases which Paul uses to confirm the fact that even in I Corinthians, the true gift is speaking in foreign languages.

6. Again in I Corinthians 14:

There are, it may be, so many kinds of languages in the world, and none of them is without significance. Therefore, if I do not know the meaning of the language, I shall be a foreigner to him who speaks, and he who speaks will be a foreigner to me (I Cor. 14:10).

Some Charismatics are upset that the New King James Version uses the word *"languages"* here because the word used here is our word for *"voice"*. We use it for *"telephone"*. Literally, it says, *"... so many languages"*. Although the word *"language"* is not used here, I believe the word *"language"* is a correct translation because in the following verse it says, *"... if I don't know the meaning of the language, I wil be a foreigner to him who speaks ...."* It's almost as if God uses the word *"foreigner"* to underscore that the word *"voice"* means foreign languages. These are not ecstatic utterances in these verses; such a translation would not make sense.

7. The association of Luke and Paul is another reason I believe the gift of tongues refers only to foreign languages. What do I mean? Luke wrote Acts. Paul wrote I Corinthians. Why would the Holy Spirit lead Luke to say the gift of tongues is foreign languages, and then have Paul say the gift of tongues is ecstatic utterances? These men were closely associated with one another. From Acts 16:10 on, Luke travelled with Paul on his missionary journeys. This association argues for unity of interpretation in their writings. The word means the same thing in Acts that it means in I Corinthians.

How can we today, at this distance, decide that they were different just so we can solve a problem? I don't believe that and I don't understand how people can argue for that when the two writers were so closely associated and could have discussed this many, many times. The true biblical gift of tongues is being able to speak in a foreign language without prior knowledge of the language.

God could give that gift to believers today, but He doesn't necessarily do so. We no longer have sacrificial systems nor do we have the gift of tongues any longer. God has the power to give that gift today. I do not question God's power. I don't believe that we can prove whether the gift of tongues has ceased or not. God **could** give people the ability to speak in languages they haven't learned today, but the argument is usually for a private prayer language. The evidence is for foreign languages as I see it. Even a strong leader (a friend of mine) in the Charismatic movement says that true speaking in tongues is rare; there is a lot of misunderstanding and counterfeiting done with this gift.

For as the body is one and has many members, but all the members of that one body, being many, are one body, so also is Christ. For by one Spirit we were all baptized into one body-whether Jews or Greeks, whether slaves or free-and have all been made to drink into one Spirit. For in fact the body is not one member but many. If the foot should say, "Because I am not a hand, I am not of the body," is it therefore not of the body? And if the ear should say, "Because I am not an eye, I am not of the body," is it therefore not of the body? If the whole body were an eye, where would be the hearing? If the whole were hearing, where would be the smelling? But now God has set the members, each one of them, in the body just as He pleased. And if they were all one member, where would the body be? But now indeed there are many members, yet one body. The eye cannot say to the hand, "I have no need of you"; nor again the head to the feet, "I have no need of you." No, much rather, those members of the body which seem to be weaker are necessary. And those members of the body which we think to be less honorable, on these we bestow greater honor; and our unpresentable parts have greater modesty, but our presentable parts have no need. But God composed the body, having given greater honor to that part which lacks it, that there should be no schism in the body, but that the members should have the same care for one another. And if one member suffers, all the members suffer with it; or if one member is honored, all the

members rejoice with it. Now you are the body of Christ, and members individually (I Cor. 12:12-27).

It's easy to emphasize our differences, but the Bible teaches us that these differences don't make more than one body, but are given to us to build up the body.

Tongues In The Church Of Corinth

Paul and Luke wrote about the Gift of Speaking in Tongues which was well known in the early church as the Apostles went from place to place talking about Jesus' life, death and resurrection. When the Apostles wrote the Epistles and when Paul wrote his letters to the churches they claimed a certain authenticity which required confirmation. The Gift of Tongues and the Gifts of Healings were given to them (as they had been given to Jesus) to confirm their message as being a message from God. *"The Jews require a sign."* So, God gave them *"signs, wonders and miracles"* as His seal of authenticity on the words spoken by these men.

In Corinth, however, there grew up an abuse, a misuse of the Gift of Tongues which Paul felt he had to deal with. On the Day of Pentecost, the Apostles had spoken foreign languages to reach the multitudes who were in Jerusalem from many parts of the world with the truth of God about Jesus. It clearly points out that each man heard in his own language (see Acts 2:8) so we are not jumping to any unwarranted conclusions. The abuse in Corinth appears to be that they were speaking something unintelligible. It was not a case of speaking foreign languages so that strangers could understand the gospel. In I Corinthians 14, we find the word *"tongue"* (singular) instead of *"tongues"* (plural) as it was used in other references.

That the Corinthian Church was carnal is another obvious fact since we read Paul's rebuke to them for their carnality and lack of maturity (see I Cor. 3:1). One of the evidences of this immaturity was their abuse of the Spiritual Gifts. It is possible for any of the Spiritual Gifts to be misused; certainly it was not strange to think that the Gift of Tongues could be misused in the Church of Corinth.

History tells us something of the situation in Corinth and it confirms that it was common among pagan religions to have ecstatic utterances. Therefore in the church, too, they were obsessed with ecstatic utterances. Pagan practices included a gibberish along with dancing and people who went into trances. The people in the Corinthian Church were familiar with such practices and incorporated them into their worship even when there was no need for foreign languages — their church was not being visited by people from all around the world at that time. Paul changed to the word *"tongue"* here to show them that this was not the same as the gift God had given. Paul had the Gift of Tongues and he spoke in many foreign languages.

This is my assessment of the situation in Corinth, but suppose I am wrong! Even if they had the true Gift of Tongues, there was still a problem in the Church of Corinth concerning this gift.

For he who speaks in a tongue does not speak to men but to God, for no one understands him; however, in the spirit he speaks mysteries (I Cor. 14:2).

I've read some commentators who do not see the negative impact of this verse. They conclude that it means that it is all right for a person to speak in tongues even when there is no one to interpret. We know from other passages, however, that Paul condemns that practice. Here, Paul is saying that they are speaking in tongues and no one knows what they are saying, but they should!

Note that the word *"spirit"* in this verse is not capitalized — that is, it does not refer to the Holy Spirit. Also, the word *"the"* does not precede it in the Greek. It actually reads, *"... in (the realm of) spirit, he speaks mysteries."* It is contrary to the Bible to say that people can speak *"mysteries"* and no one needs to understand them. It is God's will that people understand the Gift of Tongues.

We have seen that the gifts were given to build up believers and without the listeners being able to understand what was said, the basic principle of church ministry was thwarted. The person mentioned in verse 2 was not ministering to other believers nor fulfilling the principle of evangelism. Hebrews 10 teaches that church gatherings are meant to be a place where Christians exhort and encourage each other.

But he who prophesies speaks edification and exhortation (counsel) and comfort to men (I Cor. 14:3).

The word *"comfort"* involves intimacy — literally it means to *"speak close"*. It was used a lot in regard to funerals where the intimacy was based on need. This kind of ministry brings joy to the hearts of believers and it makes this comment vital to the passage. It is saying that when you use a Spiritual Gift, you accomplish three things — edification, exhortation and comfort. It is well for us to evaluate our own use of the Spiritual Gift God has given us and see if we are exercising it in intimacy and tenderness. Do you draw near to the heart of those to whom you minister?

... as you know how we exhorted, and comforted, and charged every one of you, as a father does his own children (I Thess. 2:11).

Now we exhort you, brethren, warn those who are unruly, comfort the fainthearted (little souls), uphold the weak, be patient with all (I Thess. 5:14).

These verses give us a picture of what ministry of the Spiritual Gifts is all about. Sadly, that is NOT what was happening in the Church at Corinth.

Those who believe that this passage is commending the use of tongues will say that the next verse is saying that the Gift of Tongues is good for private edification and this is only a comparison between two gifts.

He who speaks in a tongue edifies himself, but he who prophesies edifies the church (I Cor. 14:4).

However you might like to interpret this verse, it must be seen in the light of the other verses which address the matter of self-edification. When you look for such support, you find that there is none. Scripture does not teach self-edification.

But the manifestation of the Spirit is given to each one for the profit of all (I Cor. 12:7).

You'll find that the words *"of all"* are in italics meaning that they are not found in the original language. The word used there is literally *"the bearing together"* of the body of Christ. It seems clear that God gives the manifestation of the Spirit to each believer for the good of the whole body. This is borne out in the rest of Chapter 12 as well as in other Scriptures.

As each one has received a gift, minister it to one another, as good stewards of the manifold grace of God (I Peter 4:10).

Spiritual gifts are given to believers in order to minister to each other. The primary purpose of the gifts is to minister to others.

... all things are lawful for me, but all things do not edify. Let no one seek his own, but each one the other's well-being (I Cor. 10:23-24).

Let each of us please his neighbor for his good, leading to edification. For even Christ did not please Himself (Rom. 15:2-3).

The Bible does not teach us to engage at length in self-help. I do not believe in the private edification of believers through the gifts. We sometimes try to understand ourselves, but God tells us that this is a futile exercise.

The heart is deceitful above all things, And desperately wicked; who can know it? I, the Lord, search the heart (Jer. 17:9-10).

It is unhealthy for us to spend our time trying to figure out who we are and what makes us behave as we do. It is a waste of God's time. Introspection makes our heads hurt ! We need to know what the Bible says about us. If what we find there is even half right, then we need Jesus! I'm not trying to put down things that have been helpful to

you; however, the Bible does not support all this self-help teaching that we hear all around us.

Christ is our example and *"He did not please himself"*. Our goal in life should not be to do what we want to do. We need to pursue the love of God and the love of others.

The passage in I Corinthians 14 continues:

> *Therefore let him who speaks in a tongue pray that he may interpret. For if I pray in a tongue, my spirit prays, but my understanding is unfruitful (I Cor. 14:13-14).*

Again, some people use this to try and say that we don't need to comprehend with our minds what the Holy Spirit is doing in us. But rightly, Paul here is rebuking that practice. In the pagan practices of that day, it was common for people to let themselves go in an emotional frenzy and I believe that the Corinthians were doing that in counterfeiting God's true Gift of Tongues. I do not believe that we can EVER check our minds off in any ministry.

> *What is the result then? I will pray with the spirit, and I will also pray with the understanding. I will sing with the spirit, and I will also sing with the understanding (I Cor. 14:15).*

Those who argue against mental comprehension say that Paul was using the gifts that way, but it doesn't follow from the original language here. The expression *"if I pray"* is one of four different "class conditions" in Greek. When they said, "If and it is true of me," they had to use a certain form. That is NOT the form used here. When they wanted to, they would state it, "If and it may or may not be true of me," and this is the form Paul used here. However, in the context, we learn that Paul did not exercise Spiritual Gifts in that manner.

What Paul says here is very important for those who take part in the music ministry of the church. Paul says that *"in the spirit"* has to do with the inner man, but it must also be done with the mind or it has no value. This passage is discussing what a person feels and it is a statement that the mind must be the controlling factor in praying and singing for the Lord. Religious experience divorced from mental comprehension is not biblical nor is it valid. It is NEVER right to feel something great from God by means of turning off your brain. It can be done, but it will be *"unfruitful"*.

The Bible teaches us to *"bring every thought into captivity to Christ"*. The renewal of the Christian's life happens in the arena of the mind. The Bible teaches us to be like Jesus in our actions and reactions. The mind feels, thinks and perceives. We usually describe these as emotions, but they come from the mind. Some people try to tell us that this exalts "the intellect", but stop and think! It is IMPOSSIBLE to separate your mind

from what you think or feel about anything. The Bible gives the correct view of what controls man - it is his mind.

Beyond all of this discussion lies the fact that in the Church of Corinth, they were using the Gift of Tongues in violation of the purpose given for that particular gift.

> *Brethren, do not be children in understanding; however, in malice be babes, but in understanding be mature. In the law it is written: "With men of other tongues and other lips I will speak to this people; And yet, for all that, they will not hear Me," says the Lord. Therefore tongues are for a sign, not to those who believe but to unbelievers (I Cor. 14:20-22).*

Paul concludes from the Lord's words that tongues are for a sign to unbelievers. The real controversy over this chapter lies in how you read it. I read it that Paul was condemning the Corinthians.

> *Therefore if the whole church comes together in one place, and all speak with tongues, and there come in those who are uninformed or unbelievers, will they not say that you are out of your mind? But if all **prophesy**, and an unbeliever or an uninformed person comes in, he is convinced by all, he is judged by all. And thus the secrets of his heart are revealed; and so, falling down on his face, he will worship God and report that God is truly among you (I Cor. 14:23-25).*

Paul says that speaking in tongues will make unbelievers think that Christians are out of their minds. However, if those same unbelievers hear us prophesying, they will be convinced of God's truth, fall on their faces and worship God, and they will report that God is among us.

The rest of this chapter deals with the problem that **all** of the Corinthians wanted to be involved in the public worship services. They all wanted to take part. We are all to minister our gifts — that's true — but we're not all to minister in the same service! Verse 26 establishes that Paul is referring to one particular occasion, and he points out that when all try to be involved at the same time, it leads to confusion and lack of order.

> *God is not the author of confusion but of peace, as in all the churches of the saints (I Cor. 14:33).*

> *Let all things be done decently and in order (I Cor. 14:10).*

It simply is not God's will for everybody to take part at the same time. The obvious point here is that in the Church of Corinth that's what they were trying to do. It caused some people to violate the Scripture in regard to the use of Spiritual Gifts.

Let your women keep silent in the churches, for they are not permitted to speak; but they are to be submissive, as the law also says. And if they want to learn something, let them ask their own husbands at home; for it is shameful for women to speak in church. Or did the word of God come originally from you? Or was it you only that it reached? (I Cor. 14:34-36).

Most women are not very encouraged when they read this. There are two main views of this passage. Obviously, Paul is saying that what they were doing in Corinth was wrong, but was he referring to speaking in tongues only? It's possible. It could be that he was referring to speaking in tongues and prophesying; however, in Chapter 11, he said that it was all right for women to prophesy under certain conditions. The other possibility is that Paul was saying that women were not to speak in public assemblies at all. Many churches today hold that view.

I have some problems with all of this. The Greek word for *"wives"* and for *"women"* is the same word. The way you tell which one is meant is by the word used for *"man"*. The word used here refers to *"husbands"*, not just men in general. We can conclude then that *"wives"* are meant in this passage.

This helps us when we come to the reference to the law. The only thing I can find in the law on this is found in Genesis 3 where God deals with the wife being submissive to her husband. Incidentally, submission is not just for women, nor just for wives. We also read, *"Submit yourselves one to another and so fulfill the law of Christ."* Just because the problem here was among the women doesn't make submission a uniquely feminine thing.

In other passages such as I Timothy 2:11-15, we find the emphasis on tranquility of heart rather than submission or silence. The idea is that a woman is to find contentment and peace of heart in her position as a wife.

Nor are we to jump to the conclusion that ALL women are to submit to ALL men! This passage refers to a woman's relationship with her own husband and does not infer a general female submission to all males.

God is very strong on the family as the backbone of society, as well as the backbone of the church of Jesus Christ and He often instructs us on how to get our families to function at their best.

Sometimes wives may know more than their husbands and have more talent, besides. Since she is not the head of the family, however, she is not to use her gifts in defiance of her husband, but in concert with his leadership.

On the other hand, I cannot support the opinion that some impose on God's Word here and conclude that no woman should **ever** have a place of ministry nor ever be permitted to speak a word.

> *Let your wives keep silent in the churches, for they are not permitted to speak (in tongues, probably), for they are to be submissive ... it is shameful for women to speak in the church (I Cor. 14:34).*

In Corinth, some wives were violating the Scripture and usurping authority over their husbands in the public assembly. This was disrupting their family life and, hence, it was disrupting the church. It was resulting in spiritual pride and ignorance, as well.

> *If anyone thinks himself to be a prophet or spiritual, let him acknowledge that the things which I write to you are the commandments of the Lord (I Cor. 14:37).*

The true gift of speaking in tongues is not to be denied; however, as with all the gifts, it is to be controlled. Two or three may speak in tongues with only one to interpret their message. There was a true Gift of Tongues.

> *Therefore, brethren, desire earnestly to prophesy, and do not forbid to speak with tongues. Let all things be done decently and in order (I Cor. 14:39-40).*

The Gift of Interpretation

In I Corinthians 12:10 we find the Interpretation of Tongues listed as a Spiritual Gift. The meaning is *"to interpret, expound, explain or translate"*. There are twenty places in the Bible where the word in its various forms is found. Seven of these refer to the Spiritual Gift. In twelve places it is used to mean "translate" or "give the meaning of names". In Luke 24:27 it is used of expounding (explaining) the Scriptures.

It is simply defined as the ability to translate for the benefit of others, the message of one who speaks in tongues without any previous knowledge of the language being spoken. The only illustration of the use of this gift in the early church is found in I Corinthians 14.

If anyone speaks in a tongue, let there be two or at the most three, each in turn, and let one interpret. But if there is no interpreter, let him keep silent in church, and let him speak to himself and to God (I Cor. 14:27-28).

The word used in regard to the Gift of Interpretation is most often found when it can only mean an exact translation. It is used of the meaning of a name, for instance, where it cannot refer to anything except an exact translation. Thus, the common use of this word leads us to believe that it does not ordinarily allow for any expounding on what was said as is the practice today. From its usage, it appears that the primary meaning would limit the interpreter to the basic meaning of what was said.

This chapter (in verses 5 and 13) also appears to allow for the possibility that one who speaks in tongues could interpret for himself.

I wish you all spoke with tongues, but even more that you prophesied; for he who prophesies is greater than he who speaks with tongues, unless indeed he interprets, that the church may receive edification (I Cor. 14:5).

Therefore let him who speaks in a tongue pray that he may interpret (I Cor. 5:13).

In the public assembly, only one person was to interpret for those who spoke in tongues. This could possibly indicate that the individual was given the ability to understand the meaning of several languages of which he had no prior knowledge (see I Cor. 14:27).

Paul left no doubt that there was to be no speaking in tongues without an interpreter present (see I Cor. 14:28).

What Is The Baptism of the Holy Spirit?

Luke wrote in Luke 24:49 and in Acts 1:4-5 quoting Jesus as calling the Holy Spirit *"the Promise of the Father"*. No doubt, this served as a reminder of what Jesus had taught the disciples about the coming of the Holy Spirit after He departed for heaven.

Luke also writes quoting Peter on the Day of Pentecost as referring to the Holy Spirit as a *"gift"*. He repeats this concept in Acts 10 and 11 when the Holy Spirit came upon the Gentiles when they received *"repentance to life"*. This amazed the Jews who had not expected to see Gentiles as a part of the Church of Jesus Christ.

The phrase *"received the Holy Spirit"* is found in Acts 10 and in Acts 19:1-5 where about twelve men had followed John's baptism but had not been baptized in the name of Jesus Christ. When they were baptized in water in Jesus' name, *"the Holy Spirit came upon them, and they spoke with tongues and prophesied."* There is no doubt that the Holy Spirit is closely tied into the experience of identifying ourselves with Jesus.

That helps when we arrive at I Corinthians 12 where the definition of *"the baptism of the Holy Spirit"* is given.

> *For by one Spirit we were all baptized into one body—whether Jews or Greeks, whether slaves or free—and have all been made to drink into one Spirit (I Cor. 12:13).*

The Apostles made it clear in their writings that Jesus Christ is the One who baptizes us with the Holy Spirit. John the Baptist said,

> *I indeed baptize you with water unto repentance, but He who is coming after me is mightier than I, whose sandals I am not worthy to carry. He will baptize you with the Holy Spirit and fire (Matt. 3:11).*

Even though John the Baptist said this at the outset of Jesus' ministry, no one saw this happen until the Day of Pentecost in Acts 2 and the days following. In each instance, it happened at the time of the person's placing their faith in Jesus Christ. It is also clear in I Corinthians that there is only *"one baptism"* of the Holy Spirit. Paul repeats this truth in Ephesians.

> *There is one body and one Spirit, just as you were called in one hope of your calling; one Lord, one faith, one baptism; one God and Father of all, who is above all, and through all, and in you all (Eph. 4:4-6).*

Discovering Your Spiritual Gift

There are a dozen points to keep in mind as you come to search for your Spiritual Gift. Each one of these concepts comes from God's Word which, in itself, makes each one essential to this process. We must use the Bible to guide us at this point, just as we have looked to His Word as our guide in learning about the Spiritual Gifts.

> *As each one has received a gift, minister it to one another, as good stewards of the manifold grace of God (I Peter 4:10).*

There can be no doubt that this verse teaches us that every one has a gift from God. Some people tend to shy away from this concept in feelings of humility and unworthiness, but God does not give His gifts on the basis of merit any more than salvation is granted only to those who are worthy. On the contrary! Salvation is for those who are needy and helpless, and God gives His gift of salvation as just that — a gift. It isn't anything we deserve or that we can earn. He gives His gift of salvation to those He chooses. Just so, Spiritual Gifts are given *"as He wills"* and we do not dictate to Him, nor sway Him toward, or away from His plan which was *"before the foundation of the earth"*. He planned all of this long before we came on the scene!

> *But the manifestation of the Spirit is given to each one for the profit of all ... But one and the same Spirit works all these things, distributing to each one individually as He wills (I Cor. 12:7, 11).*

Next, we must understand that the Holy Spirit is the One who has given us the gift He wanted us to have. These things are an expression of Him and He has a plan to use His gifts to build the church of Jesus Christ. There is no credit to attend to the person who receives the gift. It is the Holy Spirit who moves to enable us to function in the body of Christ. Without Him, we would have no power or ability to be useful at all.

We've spent a considerable amount of time now getting to know the purpose of the gifts so that we can see it work in our lives to the fullest. Since there is such a diversity of gifts as well as a variety of ways in which they can be used, we need to be clear in our thinking as to the purpose for which the Holy Spirit has given us our gift. This helps us to use it according to the guidelines of Scripture and keeps us from wandering around in the dark.

> *Pursue love, and desire spiritual gifts, but especially that you may prophesy ... Even so you, since you are zealous for spiritual gifts, let it be for the edification of the church that you seek to excel (I Cor. 14:1, 12).*

It is scriptural to desire to know what your gift is and to want to make the most of it. The warning inherent in these verses, however, is that we be motivated *"for the edification of the church"*. Too many among us are seeking to find our personal worth in the gift that God has given us instead of seeking to build His church by its exercise.

We have intrinsic worth in the eyes of God. We don't have any **added** worth because of the gift the Holy Spirit gives us. God loved us enough to sacrifice His Son — that tells us what we are worth. Self-esteem is not to be found in what we can do, or in the position we occupy although that's where we all seem to look for it. God paid the supreme sacrifice for us BEFORE we ever knew Him. We can't add anything to that no matter what gift we have. Still, for the good of the believers, we are allowed — even encouraged to know what our gift is and to use it wisely.

Remember, too, that the Holy Spirit is to have a bigger part in our lives than just the bestowing of a Spiritual Gift. He is to control and dominate us so that Jesus Christ may be honored.

> *Do not be drunk with wine, in which is dissipation; but be filled with the Spirit, speaking to one another in psalms and hymns and spiritual songs, singing and making melody in your heart to the Lord, giving thanks always for all things to God the Father in the name of our Lord Jesus Christ, submitting to one another in the fear of God (Eph. 5:18-21).*

Wine does not follow the digestive tract as food does. It spreads out into the body going through the walls of the stomach and into every part by that means. Just so the Holy Spirit is to permeate our hearts and minds, taking control of us until we no longer exercise our own wills, but do His will completely.

This includes leaving the work of the Holy Spirit up to Him. We're relieved of striving to have a place of influence and can allow the love of God to be expressed in tangible ways.

> *It is God who works in you both to will and to do for His good pleasure (Phil. 2:13).*

God's work done in God's way accomplishes the things He planned. We'll be surprised with what comes of most of our enterprises. Most of the time we don't have much of a clue as to what God has in mind.

When you have an interest in a certain gift, or if you want to take part in God's work in a special way, then you can consider that to be a factor needing to be taken into account. Other people may not see that gift in you at first; however, a strong desire for a certain gift may be the first indication that it is the gift the Holy Spirit has given to you.

Delight yourself also in the Lord, And He shall give you the desires of your heart (Ps. 37:4).

It follows then, that you will make yourself available to use the gift you believe you have been given. Now is the time to remember that ALL of the gifts are tied to God and His Word. They must be used within the parameters that God has set. We are not to strike out on our own to do what we think God wants done, but are to check ourselves against God's Word again and again.

As each one has received a gift, minister it to one another, as good stewards of the manifold grace of God. If anyone speaks, let him speak as the oracles of God. If anyone ministers, let him do it as with the ability which God supplies, that in all things God may be glorified through Jesus Christ, to whom belong the glory and the dominion forever and ever. Amen (I Peter 4:10-11).

One aspect we see in these verses is that we are to work authoritatively. When we speak God's words, we don't rely on our own authority, but His. When glory is to be assigned, it goes to God.

A corroborating element is the wisdom and advice that mature believers and church leaders can give you. These people are tuned into the Holy Spirit and tend to see things in that light. If there is a strong indication from them that the gift you're using is blessed of the Holy Spirit, you can see that as confirmation that you are pursuing your gift properly and wisely. However, if these spiritual leaders let you know that your ministry is not effective, it is time to review what you have considered to be your gift and explore other gifts until you are sure of the Holy Spirit's direction in your life.

This kind of evaluation should only come after continual use of your gift and after you have reached a good level of maturity in your own life. Then, you will be strong enough to seek the wisdom and advice of others and you will have the courage to implement what they tell you about yourself. Sometimes we are the last ones to understand ourselves and God's leading in our lives.

It is important, too, to accept God's chain of command such as the relationships in marriage and the family, church leadership, business positions, and school or government administration. These patterns are governed by Scripture and God has set them in place in your life for His reasons. If you ignore these positions and authorities, you will be going contrary to God's Word and will suffer the resulting lack of blessing. Using your gift is going to fit within these parameters, not cross these lines. God's will for your life will utilize the relationships He has given in your life.

Wives, submit to your own husbands, as to the Lord (Eph. 5:22).

Children, obey your parents in the Lord, for this is right (Eph. 6:1).

Servants, be obedient to those who are your masters according to the flesh, with fear and trembling, in sincerity of heart, as to Christ (Eph. 6:5).

... be subject to rulers and authorities, to obey (Titus 3:1).

Remember those who rule over you, who have spoken the word of God to you, whose faith follow, considering the outcome of their conduct (Heb. 13:7).

Obey those who rule over you, and be submissive, for they watch out for your souls, as those who must give account (Heb. 13:17).

Finally, I would emphasize that we must not allow ourselves to fall into the common trap of exalting the gift more than the Giver. Too often, we are enraptured by the ability that God has placed in our lives to the point that we forget to give God the glory. This should never be the case with you and me.

Therefore, whether you eat or drink, or whatever you do, do all to the glory of God (I Cor. 10:31).

If anyone speaks, let him speak as the oracles of God. If anyone ministers, let him do it as with the ability which God supplies, that in all things God may be glorified through Jesus Christ, to whom belong the glory and the dominion forever and ever. Amen (I Peter 4:11).

Three Keys to Discovering Your Gift

Desire

What gifts would you like to see developed in your life?

If a man desires the position of a bishop,
he desires a good work (I Tim. 3:1).

Pursue love, and desire spiritual gifts, but especially
that you may prophesy (I Cor. 14:1).

Delight yourself also in the Lord, And He shall give
you the desires of your heart (Ps. 37:4).

Joy

What gifts bring you the most joy in thinking
about them and in using them?

I am being poured out as a drink offering on the sacrifice
and service of your faith, I am glad and rejoice with you all.
For the same reason you also be glad and rejoice with me (Phil. 2:17-18).

Rejoice in the Lord always. Again I will say, rejoice! (Phil 4:4).

Effectiveness

What gifts have you found to be effective
in terms of results and in the eyes of others?

Even so you, since you are zealous for spiritual gifts, let it be
for the edification of the church that you seek to excel (I Cor. 14:12).

For I long to see you, that I may impart to you some spiritual gift,
so that you may be established—that is, that I may be encouraged
together with you by the mutual faith both of you and me (Rom. 1:11-12)

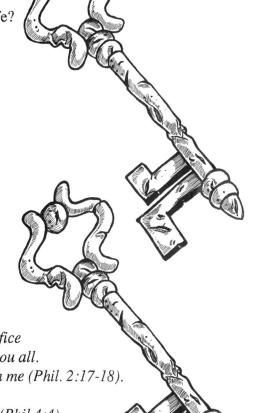

Discovering Your Spiritual Gift

NOTE: Mark "Yes" (Y) in the lefthand margin for each question which fits you:

1. Would you describe yourself as an effective public speaker?
2. Do you find it relatively easy and enjoyable to spend time in intense study and research of the Bible?
3. Do you enjoy sharing the personal and emotional problems of people?
4. Do you find yourself more concerned with how to apply God's Word than in simply trying to understand its message?
5. Have you sensed that God has given you a special ability to learn and acquire knowledge concerning His Word?
6. Do you enjoy motivating others to various tasks and ministries?
7. Would other people describe you as a person who makes decisions easily?
8. Do you seem to concentrate more on practical things that need to be done rather than on why they should be done?
9. When you hear of someone who needs help, do you immediately offer your services if it is possible?
10. Would you rather give money to help than to perform some manual task?
11. Do you enjoy visiting people who are sick or disabled?
12. Is your home the kind that most people feel comfortable in and will often drop by to visit with you unannounced?
13. Do you find that you have the ability to believe things that other believers cannot seem to accept or see?
14. Have other believers told you that you always seem to know whether something is right or wrong?
15. When situations are not right, do you feel a burden to speak up about them in order to correct them?
16. Do you love to deal with issues and questions?
17. Have you found that people often seek you out to have your advice about their personal problems?
18. Do you find that you often know immediately what to do in a situation where other believers are not clear as to what should be done?
19. Do you find that people will often come to you with difficult problems and questions from the Bible, seeking your understanding?
20. Do you find yourself setting goals and objectives for yourself and your ministry as a believer?
21. Do you sense a great deal of responsibility to make decisions in behalf of others?
22. Do you usually have a great deal of joy in just "doing things" that need to be done no matter how small or trivial the task?
23. Do you sense a special ministry to help other people become more effective in their work?
24. When you hear of someone in need, do you immediately think of sending them some money?
25. When you hear of someone in the hospital, does it challenge you to bring them some encouragement and cheer?
26. Do you feel that something is really missing in your life when you cannot have guests into your home?
27. When people say that something cannot be done or is impossible, do you feel the burden to believe it and trust God for it?
28. Do you seem to have an understanding of people and their motivations that proves to be correct, even though you do not know them well?
29. Do you have a tendency to speak up when issues are being dealt with in a group, rather than remain silent and listen?
30. When you hear a question or problem, are you anxious to both find and give an answer?
31. Would you prefer to talk personally with someone about their problems rather than to send them to someone else for help?
32. Do people often seek your advice in difficult situations as to what you would do or how you would handle things?

33. In your study of God's Word have you observed that new insights and understanding of difficult subjects seem to come to you easily?
34. When someone is not doing a job well, do you feel concerned to help him become more effective in what he is doing?
35. Do you sense a moral responsibility when giving direction and guidance to others, always thinking of how this will affect others?
36. Do you seem to have more satisfaction in doing a task than in what others thought of what you did?
37. Do you see yourself more in a supportive ministry to others than in being in a place of leadership?
38. Do you find yourself looking for opportunities to give your money without hearing any appeals?
39. Do you find it easy to express joy in the presence of those who are suffering physically?
40. Do you love to entertain people in your home regardless of how well you know them?
41. Do you find that you usually feel opposed to anyone who expresses that something cannot be done or accomplished?
42. Do you sense often that what is being said is produced by the devil rather than God, and has your judgment proved to be correct?
43. Have you sensed that people feel conviction about wrong practices or doctinal error when you share with them what the Bible says?
44. Have people often said to you that you have an ability to explain difficult problems to them, usually giving reasons for what you believe?
45. Do you really get much joy out of encouraging people who are going through personal problems and trials?
46. Do you find that people usually ask what you think about a situation with the belief that you will always know what to do?
47. Have you noticed that you have the ability to understand difficult teachings of God's Word without a great volume of research and study?
48. Would you rather show someone else how to do a task than to do it yourself?
49. Do you enjoy giving direction to others and making decisions for them?
50. Is it true of you that when you are asked to do a particular task you usually feel no pressure or obligation?
51. Do you feel a special burden to relieve others of their duties in order to free them to do their most important work?
52. Do you find yourself responding immediately to financial needs by giving your money without a great deal of planning?
53. Is it easy for you to talk with those who are suffering physically and to experience response on their part?
54. Do you consider your home to be a real place of ministry to others?
55. Have you discovered that you do not have to wait for clear evidence and direction before you make a decision?
56. Do you find that you often evaluate people and the things they say as to whether it is right or wrong?
57. When you speak God's Word do you usually think of how this is going to challenge and motivate those to whom you are speaking?
58. Have people expressed to you how much they appreciate the way you explain things from the Bible?
59. Do you find it easy to deal with people who are depressed or discouraged, experiencing a certain joy in what can be accomplished?
60. Have other believers referred to decisions you have made or advice you have given as being the right thing to do and the best for everyone?
61. Do you seem to understand things about God's Word that other believers with the same background and experience don't seem to know?
62. Do you have a special concern to train and disciple other believers to become leaders?

63. Do you find yourself constantly thinking of decisions that need to be made in giving overall direction to a group or organization?

64. Would you rather do a job yourself than work with a group in trying to acocmplish it?

65. Do you believe that you would help almost anyone who had a need, if it were possible for you to do so?

66. Do you sense a great deal of joy in giving, regardless of the response of the one to whom you gave?

67. Do you often think of ways to minister and help those who are suffering physically?

68. Would you like to have a regular ministry of entertaining people in your home regardless of who they are?

69. Do you feel that you are able to trust God in difficult circumstances without hesitation or indecision?

70. Do you feel a great responsiblity toward God whenever you sense that something is not right which other believers do not seem to understand?

71. Have other believers shared with you that you have the ability to communicate God's Word with great effectiveness?

72. Do people come to you often, seeking your answers to specific questions or problems from the Bible?

73. Do you sense a great deal of love and compassion for people having personal and emotional problems?

74. When you give your advice to someone, do you seem to emphasize more in the area of "how" it should be done rather than "why" it should be done?

75. Have other believers frequently pointed out to you that you have an ability to know and understand the things of God's Word?

76. Do you have a special concern for people in helping them to reach their goals and objectives in their lives?

77. Do people seem to depend upon you to make the major decisions for the group or the organization?

78. When you hear of a specific job that needs to be done, are you anxious to do it yourself?

79. Are you satisfied more with how a person has been helped by what you did, than by simply doing it?

80. When you give your money to someone or something, do you usually desire to avoid letting others know what you did?

81. Would you enjoy a regular ministry to those who are suffering physically?

82. Do you look at having people into your home as an exciting ministry more than the fact that you have a responsibility to do this?

83. Have other believers often shared with you that you seem to have the ability to trust God in difficult situations?

84. Have people often asked your opinion of someone or something that has been said as to whether you thought it was right or wrong?

85. Do you believe that you have gifts in communicating to others?

86. Would you rather explain the meaning of a word than simply share a verse by quoting it to someone?

87. Do you usually desire to hear others share their personal problems rather than being able to share yours with someone else?

88. Do other believers seem to follow your advice in difficult situations?

89. Have you found in studying God's Word that you seem to know what a passage is saying before other believers discover it?

90. Do you usually take the leadership in a group where none exists?

91. Do you usually feel morally responsible for the long-range effects of your decisions?

92. Would you rather do a particular job than spend time talking with people about their problems and needs?

93. When someone asks for your help, do you have great difficulty in saying "No" to that person?

94. When you give some money to someone, do you find that you do not expect any appreciation in return?

95. Do you feel a great deal of compassion toward those who are suffering physically that makes you want to help them in some way?

96. Do you find that you can easily have people into your home without being overly concerned about how it looks?

97. Do you feel a burden to encourage people to trust God when you see them defeated and discouraged?

98. Have you felt a special responsiblity to protect the truth of God's Word by exposing that which is wrong and sinful?

99. Would you rather speak God's Word to others without much explanation than take the time to explain every detail?

100. Do you usually organize your thoughts in a systematic way?

101. When you hear of some believer who has "sinned" or "fallen away", are you anxious to go to them immediately and try to help them?

102. Have the decisions and the advice you have given in difficult situations proven to be the right thing to do in most cases?

103. Do you have a great desire to share with other believers what the meaning of a difficult verse or passage is?

104. Do you sense a great deal of joy in a leadership position, rather than frustration and difficulty?

105. Have you had experience in being responsible to make decisions in behalf of a group or organization that would affect everyone?

106. Do you find that you enjoy things that need to be done without being asked to do them?

107. Do you find yourself looking for opportunities to help other people?

108. Do you see the matter of giving money as a tremendous spiritual ministry and one which you believe God has given to you?

109. Do you find that when visiting those who are suffering physically it brings you joy rather than depressing you?

110. Have other believers often referred to your ability to have people in your home and to the way God has used you in this?

111. Have you seen God do mighty things in your life that other believers said could not be done but which you believed He would do?

112. Do you feel that you are helping other believers when you discern that something is wrong, and have they readily accepted your evaluation?

113. When an opportunity is give you to speak to other believers, do you find that you would rather share verses than to share your personal experiences?

114. Have other believers told you often that you should have a regular teaching ministry and have you felt the same?

115. Do you enjoy a person-to-person ministry more than ministering to a group?

116. Have you sensed a special ability in your life to know what to do when dealing with difficult problems and situations?

117. When you see other believers confused and lacking in understanding about some difficult teaching of the Bible, have you sensed a responsibility to speak to them about what it means?

118. Do you seem to know how to meet people's needs, goals, and desires without too much study and planning?

119. Do you enjoy being the "final voice" or the one with the overall responsibility for the direction and success of a group or organization?

120 Do you find that it is not necessary for you to have a "job description" when you are asked to do a particular task?

121. Have people often expressed to you how you have helped them in doing a particular job that relieved them of that responsiblity in order to do something else?

122. Are you really excited when someone asks you to help financially in some worthwhile project, seeing this as a great honor and privilege?

123. Are you willing and eager to spend time, money, and resources, in order to help those who are suffering physically?

124. Do you find a great joy in having people into your home rather than sensing that it is a burden or responsibility that will entail too much work?
125. Have you discovered an effective prayer ministry in your life with many wonderful answers to prayer that from a human point of view seem impossible or unlikely?
126. Have you often made an evaluation of someone or something that was said that others did not see, but yet proved to be correct?

Now that your test is over, take a moment to thank the Lord for His direction and guidance and ask Him to give you a submissive heart and a humble attitude toward whatever gift (or gifts) He has given you. Also, remember that whatever gifts we have have already been given to us the moment we became believers in Christ. Our ability to discover these gifts is based on our maturity in Christ, our continual use of these gifts, and the effectiveness and joy we have experienced when using them. Since these things change throughout our Christian experience, you will want to review the gifts often and perhaps take the test again in the future and compare those results with what you have discovered at this point.

Your "Yes" answers will serve to help you identify your gift. Circle the number for each question you answered "Yes" in the appropriate place on the list below. The area where you have the most "Yes" answers is your gift. If there is more than one gift in which you have lots of positive answers, the final answer can be found in your own attitude toward those gifts in which you scored more or less equally. God gives us a delight and satisfaction in doing His will in our lives. The Holy Spirit will guide you in the use of your gifts - rely on Him!

PROPHECY	WORD OF WISDOM	ADMINISTRATION	GIVING	FAITH
# 1	# 4	# 7	# 10	# 13
# 15	# 18	# 21	# 24	# 27
# 29	# 32	# 35	# 38	# 41
# 43	# 46	# 49	# 52	# 55
# 57	# 60	# 63	# 66	# 69
# 71	# 74	# 77	# 80	# 83
# 85	# 88	# 91	# 94	# 97
# 99	# 102	# 105	# 108	# 111
# 113	# 116	# 119	# 122	# 125

TEACHING	WORD OF KNOWLEDGE	SERVING	SHOWING MERCY
# 2	# 5	# 8	# 11
# 16	# 19	# 22	# 25
# 30	# 33	# 36	# 39
# 44	# 47	# 50	# 53
# 58	# 61	# 64	# 67
# 72	# 75	# 78	# 81
# 86	# 89	# 92	# 95
# 100	# 103	# 106	# 109
# 114	# 117	# 120	# 123

EXHORTATION	LEADERSHIP	HELPS	HOSPITALITY	DISCERNMENT
# 3	# 6	# 9	# 12	# 14
# 17	# 20	# 23	# 26	# 28
# 31	# 34	# 37	# 40	# 42
# 45	# 48	# 51	# 54	# 56
# 59	# 62	# 65	# 68	# 70
# 73	# 76	# 79	# 82	# 84
# 87	# 90	# 93	# 96	# 98
# 101	# 104	# 107	# 110	# 112
# 115	# 118	# 121	# 124	# 126